Love, Hope, Optimism

Love, Hope, Optimism

An informal portrait of
JACK LAYTON
by those who knew him

EDITED BY
JAMES L. TURK AND CHARIS WAHL

JAMES LORIMER & COMPANY LTD., PUBLISHERS
TORONTO

James Lorimer & Company Ltd., Publishers acknowledges the support of the Ontario Arts Council. We acknowledge the financial support of the Government of Canada through the Canada Book Fund for our publishing activities. We acknowledge the support of the Canada Council for the Arts which last year invested $24.3 million in writing and publishing throughout Canada. We acknowledge the Government of Ontario through the Ontario Media Development Corporation's Ontario Book Initiative.

Front cover image courtesy of Bruce Kirby
Back cover images courtesy of Doris Layton, Debbie Field,
    Susan Baker, Bruce Kirby

Library and Archives Canada Cataloguing in Publication

    Love, hope, optimism : an informal portrait of Jack Layton by those who knew him / edited by James L. Turk and Charis Wahl ; foreword by Ed Broadbent.

Issued also in an electronic format.
ISBN 978-1-4594-0264-5

    1. Layton, Jack, 1950-2011. 2. Politicians--Canada--Biography.
I. Turk, James, 1943- II. Wahl, Charis

FC641.L39L68 2012   971.07'3092   C2012-903771-0

James Lorimer & Company Ltd., Publishers
317 Adelaide Street West, Suite 1002
Toronto, ON, Canada
M5V 1P9
www.lorimer.ca

Printed and bound in Canada.

Contents

3   WALKING THE WALK

4 A MAN FOR THE COUNTRY

Foreword

ED BROADBENT

All politicians inherit their times. Then leaders begin to shape them.

When Jack Layton became leader of the NDP in 2003, the party was in distant fourth place in our national politics. When he died so tragically after four elections, during which the NDP was the only party to make four successive gains both in seats and popular vote, he did so as the Official Opposition leader. This outcome was neither a fluke nor the product of some swing of a pendulum to the left. Nor was it simply the result of the inadequacy of leaders of some other parties. Nor, in particular, was it enough that a large social democratic gap had emerged in the last campaign in Quebec after the collapse of the Bloc Québécois. These, and other causes of the NDP's rise that may be found in the future by historians, did play their roles. But the crucial element in all of the mix was Jack Layton. It was the Jack Layton I came to know closely and directly after he became leader.

It was Jack's pragmatism over a decade in the midst of egocentric and power-driven politics in Ottawa that made a minority Parliament not only work but work in a progressive direction. It was his powerful disposition not to outshine in partisan debates but to get things done that filled the gap left by the bickering in the Commons.

Canadians took notice. It was his and his staff's equally determined organizational outreach over a decade to rebuild the party in Quebec that mattered. Most notably, however, it was the pre-election reach of Jack's unpretentious warmth into the hearts of so many Quebecers via popular television that mattered so much. Then, during the French debate at the time when they were so massively rejecting an ossified Bloc Québécois, there was Jack—quick, progressive, and polite. Bringing social democracy with a warm smiling face, he provided to Quebec and the rest of Canada that most important gift of democratic leadership, a sense of hope. The right times, yes. But also very much the right leader.

Most of what follows in this book consists of personal recollections based on aspects of life shared with Jack. Mine are those of a friendship that really began after he became leader. Although I had strongly supported his leadership bid, my support was largely based on the study of his highly positive work in municipal politics. During those days in Toronto you could see what later emerged in the House of Commons—a highly energetic, practical, and innovative man, successfully implementing a progressive agenda. The important qualities of character that produced such success became apparent to me only after I joined him in caucus during 2004–6 and subsequently during his remaining years as leader as we met, more often than not over warm and engaging dinners.

Jack was fiercely ambitious for the party. Like J. S. Woodsworth and Tommy Douglas he rightly saw that winning the debate in Parliament was only the first step in politics. Winning power was what mattered. Then you could make progressive change a reality. He was determined to see an NDP federal government in his lifetime. Only then could we be assured that Canada would live up to its full potential for social justice.

En route to power Jack used his time in minority governments to get things done. He worked with prime ministers, with Stephen Harper and before that with Paul Martin, to make progressive change. He took real risks, not always getting what he wanted. But he and the caucus made real gains for seniors, the environment, and the unemployed. Compromise with a social purpose was leadership, not opportunism. Firm in his core values of compassion, tolerance, and nonviolence, he fought for housing for the poor, equality for gays and lesbians, and a gun registry that mattered. By the time of his death, whatever their partisan affiliation, Canadians had come to believe once again, however briefly, in the possibility of politics. For Jack, his final days were remarkably courageous and graceful. For the rest of us they were at once sad and uplifting.

Introduction

JAMES L. TURK

The last time I saw Jack was at a campaign speech he gave in Gatineau, Quebec in the midst of the 2011 federal election. As a perennial pessimist about the likelihood of progressive change, I had gone to the NDP's rally with my son Alexi to see first-hand if the rumours of the orange wave spreading across Quebec were true. Secretly, I feared the rumours were mostly wishful thinking but, if so, at least Alexi and I would add two more bodies to help fill up the room.

It was a gray April day, with storms threatening, and the location was in what seemed a remote suburb that I found thanks only to my cellphone's GPS. My worst fears seemed ready to unfold. But there in the school's parking lot was the NDP campaign bus with an enormous picture of a radiant Jack Layton—enough to lift any New Democrat's spirits. Even better, the parking lot was jammed. When Alexi and

I went in, the hall was overflowing and, even though we were quite early, we had to find standing room in one of the doorways.

The crowd erupted when Jack entered. He was in fine form, with no hint of the pain he was suffering or the disease that would claim him in less than four months. He had transformed the only visible sign of health problems, his cane, into a drum major's baton that became a symbol of strength, enthusiasm, and determination.

Following his talk, he was thronged by supporters who wanted to shake his hand, tell him of their support, or give him a bit of advice. As he made his way slowly to the exit (the doorway where Alexi and I were standing), Jack looked over, saw me, and made his way over. He gave me a big hug, asked about my family and me, and said how much he appreciated the work my daughter Jessica was doing as a senior member of his staff. This was pure Jack—surrounded by hundreds of people and loads of media, he created a space as if I were the only person in his world. I introduced him to Alexi, whom he had not met. Jack gave him a big hug and had the same kind of personal conversation with him before moving on.

Jack was a politician who broke the stereotype of "politician." He did not glad-hand; he engaged. He was not one thing in public and something very different in private. His interest in people was genuine, and they could feel it. That was brought home to me when I went to his funeral and walked through Nathan Phillips Square, the huge public space in front of Toronto City Hall that is paved with thousands of large concrete squares. Even though it was widely reported at the time, the scene was unbelievable. Every concrete square was filled with chalked messages about Jack, as was virtually every inch of every other surface in front of city hall. Thousands had brought flowers, wreaths, mementoes, photos, and signs, transforming the east side of Nathan Phillips Square into a popular shrine to Jack.

When I commented on the thousands of messages, someone pointed out that there had been a big rainstorm the day before that had washed everything away, but that the square had been filled with new messages in less than twenty-four hours. So many began: "I was never interested in politics before you," "I've never voted NDP but you have changed how I think about politics," and "Thanks Jack, we'll miss you." Thousands of ordinary Canadians took the unprecedented step of showing their respect for a politician in an age when the regard for politicians typically ranks alongside used-car salespeople.

So I was delighted when Jim Lorimer and his editorial director, Diane Young, asked if I would be interested in editing a book of remembrances about Jack. The project has been more fascinating than I ever expected.

Jack was a man of many interests—the environment, poverty, housing, equity, justice, municipal governance, and labour rights, to name a few. As I talked with possible contributors to this book from these different worlds, each saw Jack as more than a supporter of their cause. They saw him as someone who was part of their particular movement; someone knowledgeable about their issues, keen to make a difference, a person prepared to go the extra mile with them regardless of his many other commitments. In short, homelessness activists saw Jack as one of them; environmentalists saw Jack as an environmentalist; those championing gay rights saw a dedicated ally; members of the food movement saw Jack as one of their own; and so on for each group or cause that Jack supported.

Jack was also an academic, who received his BA in political science at McGill University and his MA and PhD in the same subject at York University. He joined the faculty of Ryerson University in 1974 and also taught at York and the University of Toronto. I first met Jack when he agreed to take over a course I was teaching on urban issues at Innis College, as I was going on leave. Jack left the academy for municipal politics in 1982, but continued as an adjunct faculty member at the University of Toronto for several years afterwards.

A man of many talents, Jack was a keen musician and skilled auctioneer who volunteered his services for any worthwhile community group that needed his help in fundraising. I remember once when he begged off from a dinner because he had to meet with a small church group that needed help fundraising for its work to aid the homeless. At the time, I was disappointed because dinners with Jack were an occasion of wide-ranging and stimulating discussion, but I also found it unusual that a politician would be so generous with a group that was not even in the ward he represented as a municipal councillor. Jack didn't think of those things. For him, it was simply a group trying to do good work that needed help. That was all he needed to know.

That tradition was bred into Jack. His great-grandfather had come to Canada as an immigrant who had worked as a piano tuner, one of the few jobs open to a blind person. He turned that into a successful retail piano business in Montreal and went on to found the Montreal Association for the Blind and the Canadian Federation for the Blind—work carried forward by the Layton family ever since. As Diane McIntyre, Jack's oldest cousin, relates in one of her contributions to this book, the family tradition was one of community service.

Politics were also bred into Jack. His grandfather, Gilbert Layton, was a member of Quebec's legislative assembly for Maurice Duplessis's Union Nationale, before quitting the party in 1939 to protest Duplessis's opposition to conscription in the Second World War. Jack's father, Robert Layton, was a cabinet minister in Brian Mulroney's Progressive Conservative government in the 1980s. Jack's first political achievement was in high school, when he was elected president of the Hudson High School student council. But even then Jack felt elected office was not an end in itself but a means to bring change. After graduation, he led an effort to build a centre for youth in Hudson, Quebec.

The joy of editing this book was the chance to talk with so many people whose lives intersected with Jack and to hear their stories about this remarkable Canadian. I was also privileged when Diane Young suggested that Charis Wahl join me as co-editor. I hope the many fascinating stories we have collected will give Canadians the opportunity to get to know Jack better through the memories of those who knew him well.

A friend to many, a politician, a musician, an academic, an auctioneer, a community activist, a dedicated family member, and a campaigner for social justice, Jack was always a big-ideas person whose many worlds were connected, often to the consternation of those who wanted him to focus more narrowly on a particular priority. As Anne McGrath describes in her contribution to this book, Jack loved absorbing ideas and discussing them—seeing wisdom in everyone. Bright, ebullient, optimistic, and enthusiastic, Jack was a force to be reckoned with—whether in endless discussions with friends and family around his and Olivia's dining room table, at a community meeting, as president of the Canadian Federation of Municipalities, or in the House of Commons.

Even during his dying hours, with the help of close friends such as Brian Topp and Anne McGrath, he wrote to his fellow Canadians, thanking them for their good wishes. He advised others with cancer not to lose hope or be discouraged that his own journey had not gone as well as he had hoped, pointing out that new therapies and treatments were better than ever. To his fellow New Democrats, he expressed his deep appreciation for their support and confidence, urging them to remain committed to their work and remembering that their cause is much bigger than any one leader. He said to young people that their energy, vision, and passion for justice were what Canada needs today, indicating his belief that they had to be at the heart of Canada's economy, political life, and plans for the present and the future. He reminded all Canadians that Canada can be a country of greater equality, justice, and opportunity and ended with the words that we felt were fitting for the title of this book: "Love is better than anger. Hope is better than fear. Optimism is better than despair. So let us be loving, hopeful and optimistic. And we'll change the world."

All royalties from this book will go to the Broadbent Institute, an initiative Jack championed as part of his life's work to help us together build a country of greater equality, justice, and opportunity with a prosperous economy and a society that shares its benefits more fairly.

1

In the Beginning

Jack Layton was born into politics. His grandfather, Gilbert, was a member of the Quebec legislature. His father, Bob, served in the Mulroney cabinet. (Politics must be in the Layton male DNA: his son Mike is a Toronto city councillor.) Born in 1950, Jack came of age in an era of activism, so it was no surprise that he saw political and social engagement as the way to tackle the inequalities he saw around him. In his early years, he spoke out about everything from bullying to better relations between the French and English inhabitants in his hometown of Hudson, Quebec.

Moving to Montreal in the late 1960s, Jack experienced large cities first-hand. As a student at McGill, and later doing graduate work and teaching in Toronto, Jack explored ways to understand the workings of this larger world, particularly its prejudices and blindspots, whether ethnic, economic, social, or environmental. As his students learned, he too developed a growing understanding of the policies, and the means of implementing them, that improved—or held back—urban life.

An Early Family Portrait
DI McINTYRE

Our great-grandfather, Philip E. Layton, immigrated to Canada with a job offer to be a church organist and choir director. When he wasn't hired because he was blind, he created his own employment, first by tuning pianos and then by establishing, with his brother Herbert, Layton Brothers Pianos. This became a successful business in Montreal with a store at the corner of Stanley and St. Catherine streets. Philip was a talented musician and composer who wrote several war-era songs, including the very patriotic "Dominion March." (Jack was one of the few family members who could pound out this march on the piano or organ.)

To give back to his community, Philip E. Layton and his wife, Alice Marion Layton, founded the Montreal Association for the Blind (MAB). They purchased land and raised money to build a school for children who were blind and to provide work and training opportunities for blind adults. (Montreal's first tag day drew small donations from hundreds of Montrealers to support this effort.) Philip went on to found the Canadian Federation for the Blind and urged parliamentary committees to establish pensions for people who were blind and unable to find work. Our grandparents carried on this work; Jack's dad, the late Hon. Robert Layton, served as chair of the MAB board; and Jack's sister Nancy continues to serve on the board.

Our grandparents were Gilbert Layton (born in Montreal) and Norah Lestelle England Layton (who moved to Montreal at age seven). My mom, Joan (Layton-McIntyre-Hurley-Negus), was the first of four children in the Layton family; Jack's dad, Robert, was next, followed by Philip and Barbara

(Layton-Elvidge). The family lived at 3556 Belmore Avenue, and later 2526 Mayfair Avenue, in Notre-Dame-de-Grâce. They all went to Montreal West High School and were very active in St. Philip's Anglican Church, where all four sang in the choir. "Jack was born at 2:30 in the afternoon under a sunny sky. The happiest day of my life," said his mother, Doris Layton. She and Uncle Bob had three more happiest days when Nancy, Rob, and David joined the family, but Jack was the test case.

During our childhood, the Laytons would gather for holiday celebrations with our grandparents, Noni and Pop (Norah and Gilbert Layton). My sister Barbara, Jack, and I were the first of the grandchildren, so we were doted on by our grandparents, aunts, and uncles, who taught us lots of games and songs.

In the summertime the extended Layton families would often have overlapping holidays at our grandparents' big, sprawling summer home near the top of Conference Hill in Knowlton, Quebec. The property was large, with a long shady laneway running from the front through to the other side of the circle road (the property has since been sold and subdivided). There were grand formal gardens at the back, huge old trees on each side of the property, a large swampy area with lots of reeds and lilies, backed by woodland. We had lots of space to play and spent happy, carefree days exploring our own wilderness, building forts, and helping tend the huge perennial garden. Our grandparents seemed to know everyone on the circle and entertained often.

We went on lots of country drives, attended country and church fairs with pony rides, and had outings to see the Brome Lake ducks. Almost every day would find us on the beach or sailing at the Brome Lake Boat Club.

By 1962, there were fourteen Layton cousins, and that big old eight-bedroom house would be very lively when all of the families converged at once. We all lived in the Montreal area or in the Eastern Townships, so we were able to get together fairly often. Each family had a couple of designated bedrooms, and the house had screened porches on three sides and a huge covered veranda in the front. The porches had ping-pong tables and a chair swing—lots of room to play on rainy days. We often gathered around the Layton Brothers piano and organ for sing-songs.

Every summer, many of us would help with a grand picnic for the Montreal Association for the Blind hosted by our grandmother. The cousins would pass sandwiches and goodies, serve tea, and escort guests on walks through the gardens and for sailing and boat rides at the Brome Lake Boat Club. This annual picnic was always an event that we looked forward to and over the years we got to know many of the guests. For years after my grandparents had moved away, neighbours on the circle continued to host this annual tradition.

Jack's parents had met on a blind date at the Brome Lake Boat Club and his maternal grandparents Connie and Jack Steeves had a summer home close by on the Brome Lake shore road between Knowlton and Foster. Jack's cousins on the Steeves side of his family, Ralph, Linda, and Randy Jones, were often there when we drove around the lake to visit. On fine days, we spent hours in the water, jumping from the dock and boating. But we were sometimes encouraged to play on the screened porch where we entertained ourselves playing lots of card games and a strange homemade game that had little wooden blocks and brass pegs and a clattering brass ball. Jack's mom remembers the game, which her dad and another man had made, as "Bagatelle." I now know that we were banished to the porch to give the adults some peace, but we didn't know that then. Jack loved being allowed to head out to explore the lake in Grampa Jack's motorboat, and looked forward to building similar memories for his grandchildren as their generation's Grampa Jack.

We all gathered for Christmas holidays with various combinations of McIntyre, Layton, and Elvidge cousins in Pointe-Claire or Cowansville and with the Steeves/Jones clan in Hudson. There was always a singsong and, as a teenager, Jack was often front and centre with his guitar—for some reason I remember him often playing "The House of the Rising Sun."

I remember gathering for Easter dinner in my grandparents' apartment on Sherbrooke Street in Montreal, where we all got to choose which piece we wanted from the giant chocolate bunny sitting in the middle of the dining-room table—a gift to Pop. The singsong here was around our Grandfather Pop playing a lovely polished Layton Brothers baby grand piano—I remember running around to "Pop Goes the Weasel." Jack's mom Doris has often said, "The Laytons had 365 reasons a year to celebrate and get together."

The Laytons and Pipers in Hudson, Quebec
JOHN PIPER

In 1948, our family moved from a 1920s Montreal apartment building on Queen Mary Road to an idyllic rural paradise called Hudson, with a population of 1,000, three churches (Anglican, United, and Roman Catholic), and two languages (French and English). We lived beside the Anglican church;

the Laytons were only six or seven homesteads away. My sister Julia and I thrived in the bilingual environment.

Our French teacher, at Hudson's elementary and high schools, was the beloved Mrs. Eileen Waldron. Both young Jack Layton and I benefited from her love of French. Jack's particular brand of French, a patois, was honed largely in Hudson, where we played sports with *les garçons du village* and picked up the French they didn't teach at school. Julia recounts a telling story about a physically handicapped schoolmate in Hudson who was constantly ridiculed by her male classmates. "It was Jack," she said, "who stood up to them and put them in their place."

For me, the strongest connections with the Laytons were with Jack's dad, Bob, and mom, Doris. They ran the Hi-C Teens, an interdenominational group at Wyman United Church, which allowed me to write music, direct a choir, and run a dance band. Bob and Doris Layton were very popular with the kids as they encouraged us all to reach for new experiences and horizons. Even though he was somewhat younger, this rubbed off on Jack.

I didn't see Jack again until we both resettled in Toronto during the urban reform days of David Crombie and John Sewell.

After the 1989 massacre at the École Polytechnique in Montreal, I witnessed Jack's unstoppable efforts to grow the White Ribbon Campaign across Canada and to more than twenty countries. His mission with all governments, private enterprises, school boards, trade unions, and thousands of groups and individuals was a forever undertaking.

Following his run for the mayoralty of Toronto, which many of our generation supported, Jack said he had his eye on the federal stage. I offered to help him in the background:

deux gars d'Hudson taking on a national challenge. By 2011, in La Belle Province, *des millions de Québécois et de Québécoises l'ont connu comme "Le Bon Jack"*—capturing him squarely as he was and remained.

The last Hudson chapter occurred in early October 2011, when Jack's ashes were buried beneath a cedar bush by his mother Doris and partner Olivia Chow in the Wyman United Church cemetery. Hundreds of Hudson families, friends, and schoolmates provided testimony to the values he learned at home, at school, and in the village, as they stood together in the pouring fall rain.

Fast Friends

RICHARD ZAJCHOWSKI

Jack and I met when we were both ten years old. Our families belonged to the Hudson Yacht Club in Hudson, Quebec, about fifty kilometres west of Montreal. It was a hot August afternoon and the yacht club was putting on a play day for all the nine- and ten-year-old kids. I went to the Catholic school in town. All the other kids my age who attended the play day were from the Protestant school, so I didn't know any of them. The boys were friendly enough but distant. The one exception was a very friendly and enthusiastic boy named Jack Layton. He included me in everything and even wanted to know more about me. Of course, I liked him right away.

I didn't see much more of Jack over the following winter but I remembered him.

The next summer, the Hudson Yacht Club was organizing its first competitive swim team. A big poster on the playground notice board announced that any kid could join. I was curious but hesitant, so I went down to the first practice to check it out. I stood outside the pool area and watched what was happening. About forty kids were swimming lengths and seemed to be having a lot of fun. And I could see that my play-day buddy Jack Layton was there too! As soon as he saw me, he got out of the water, came over to greet me, and heartily encouraged me to join the team, so I did. This was the beginning of our friendship and the beginning of our love of competitive swimming.

We had a lot in common besides swimming. We were both good students and interested in all sorts of things. Our birthdays were very close—I was six days older than Jack—and birthdays were very important in competitive swimming. Young swimmers are grouped by age, so Jack and I would always be competing against each other. This didn't bother either of us; in fact it added to our friendship—we became fast friends and fast competitors. We would spend all our summer days hanging around the pool. Just like hockey-crazy kids, both of us would get inspired by our heroes, the great swimmers of our day. We spent many an hour working on streamlining our strokes and trying to mimic all the other things the greats were doing.

At the beginning of that first summer on the team I had a secret weak spot: I could not dive. Jumping in the water was fine, but diving—no way. It was embarrassing, because all the other kids could do it well. One day in practice we all had to dive off the starting block and I knew I would be caught out. I completely flubbed my dive in front of all of the team and was mortified. I got out of the water and slumped, ashamed, behind one of the pool filters. After the practice, Jack marched over to me and said, "Let's work on getting that dive right. You are a fast swimmer—you need to have a fast dive." (Jack's dive was great, of course—he seemed to be good at everything!) He spent hours working with me on diving head-first into the water. When I finally got it, I was relieved and excited, but I think Jack was even more excited than I was.

In the summer of 1964, our taskmaster swim coach had the Hudson swim team doing two practices a day—one at 11 AM and the other at the ungodly hour of 7 AM. Early in the morning, about twenty boys and girls would sleepily bicycle down to early practice, our bathing suits under our shorts. We arrived early because our coach had a rule that whoever was not in the water by 7 AM would have to go home! He was fed up with folks taking way too long to get into the pool.

Each morning as the clock ticked closer to seven, everyone threw off their clothes and hopped quickly into the water. Jack and I had a close friend, Bruce, who would often wait until the very last minute to get into the water. One morning, seconds before 7 AM, Bruce whipped down his shorts as usual, only to realize he had forgotten to put his bathing suit on! He froze for a split second before quickly pulling his shorts up. The whole team, of course, laughed uproariously.

About a week later we were again at morning swim practice before 7 AM and Jack was recounting the story of how Bruce had forgotten his bathing suit. Bruce didn't really mind because Jack wasn't being nasty—Jack just loved to set up a story with a great punchline. Seven AM was fast approaching and the coach was warning us to get into the water. Jack finished the story with only a few seconds to spare, threw his shirt off, stripped off his shorts, and raced to the edge of the pool. He was three steps into his dash for the water when he realized that he too had forgotten to put his bathing suit on! Jack dove in, but the damage had been done. When we eventually stopped laughing, the coach threw Jack his shorts, he wiggled into them, and practice began.

Like a Duck to Water
DORIS LAYTON

When Jack was ten, he approached me with the news that, as the Hudson Yacht Club had just added a swimming pool with a young man from McGill as the manager, they were going to have a swim team. The practices were to be very early and he would like to be included. I gave him an alarm clock and permission to get himself up and ride his bike there every morning. He would return for breakfast, then go back to help clean the pool and swim until noon; later, he'd go back to the pool again after adult swim. He was joined by a number of other children and had a wonderful active summer, including competing in the Canadian national age-group championship.

The parents arranged for the team members to continue training during the winter through a membership in the Montreal Amateur Association. We mothers delivered them to the commuter train after school. As their sessions were in the evening, the fathers took turns driving them home. Jack was given rules: he could continue this routine as long as his schoolwork came first, his piano practice for the music-school exams came second, and swimming third. He became very organized and remained so for the rest of his life.

He continued competing until, at fifteen, he broke the Canadian record for individual medley in the national competition. Following that, he decided that, as his times were not good enough to compete in the coming Olympics, he would take some time off and run for president of his Hudson High School student council—the start of his political career. But he always loved swimming: at McGill, he joined his swimming friends on the water polo team. Later in life, he and Olivia took a yearly holiday to the Caribbean so he could snorkel and relax in the water with the amazing sea creatures.

Idealism and Realpolitik
RICHARD ZAJCHOWSKI

Once Jack became famous as leader of the NDP I would, on occasion, feel compelled to defend his honour against the common refrain of "he's a politician and just in it for himself." I knew that Jack's desire to see a better community that worked for everyone was very real and had been woven into his character.

Jack's idealism was similar to his dad's. When we were teenagers, Mr. Layton (as we called him) set up a Sunday night youth group called The Infusers in the hall of Hudson's United Church. Although Mr. and Mrs. Layton ran the United Church Sunday school, this group was meant to be nondenominational. And it wasn't preachy: rather the focus was on "infusing" values by exploring and discussing issues of concern to youth. Each Sunday evening Mr. Layton would introduce a single topic with a movie or presentation followed by small- and large-group discussions. The evening would typically end with the singing of folk songs. (By then Jack had learned how to play guitar quite well and would accompany us.) The Infusers was very popular among Hudson teenagers because Mr. Layton didn't shy away from

controversial subjects. Drugs, alienation, sex, and the growing war in Vietnam were typical Sunday night topics.

The Infusers had another interesting service aspect to it
as well. Mr. Layton arranged trips to the Mission Hall in
downtown Montreal where we would serve Thanksgiving or
New Year's dinner to some of the less fortunate residents of
the city. For teenagers coming from a comfortable suburban
community like Hudson, this experience was somewhat
jarring. I know that on these trips Jack was particularly
struck by the inequity of people's situations in life. Jack
would often remark that "people in Hudson just don't realize how lucky they are."

Jack, like his dad, combined idealism with pragmatic
activism. They both passionately believed that helping to
build healthy community structures would allow individuals
to flourish and make the community stronger. And they
both had a very strong ethic of service to others together
with outgoing, friendly personalities. So both realized that
getting meaningful change to occur in society would involve
at least some measure of political work.

But Jack was even more idealistic than his dad. We grew
up in the sixties and all of us were steeped in "peace and
love." But Jack, more than the rest of us, really wanted to
see it happen. So he got involved.

In 1966 he was elected student council president in high
school. He pushed hard for a youth centre in Hudson and
even managed to get architectural plans drawn up. The
next year he was elected junior commodore of the then
English-only Hudson Yacht Club. Jack found out that, as
junior commodore, he could sign in as many guests to the
weekly junior dance as he wished. So on one of the dance
nights Jack got the word out that he would sign in any of

Hudson's French-speaking youth who arrived at the Yacht Club gate. A wonderful time was had by all of us, but the next day there was hell to pay. The Yacht Club directors were furious about the presence of so many French guests. Jack resigned as junior commodore before they could even call him to account.

In 1968 Jack and I got very caught up in Trudeaumania. At the time, Jack's dad was heavily involved in the Liberal Party at both the provincial and federal levels and arranged for us to do volunteer work with the local Liberal candidate. So that summer we stuffed envelopes, put up campaign posters, and did other odd jobs around the campaign office. When both Trudeau and our local candidate won, Jack and I felt like we had contributed to that win in our small way. Jack continued on in the politics of change. In both 1969 and 1970 he was elected prime minister of the Quebec Youth Parliament. Under his leadership that model parliament passed a number of progressive motions such as pay equity for women, legalization of abortion, and universal daycare.

Then came June 1972. Bob Layton sought the nomination to become the local Liberal candidate in the federal election that would take place that fall. In a way it really was his turn—he had done so much work for so many other Liberal candidates. And he was popular in the riding. The nomination meeting was held on a beautiful Sunday afternoon. Lots of us, including Jack and myself, had joined the Liberal Party and were going to vote for Bob Layton. This was pretty exciting and it looked as if Bob was going to win. He led on the first ballot and then increased his lead on the second ballot. But no candidate yet had a majority, so it came down to a third ballot.

And then the unthinkable happened. Pretty well all the defeated candidates went against Bob Layton, publicly joining hands with the one other remaining candidate. We were stunned. Some kind of backroom deal had obviously been arranged, and Bob lost the Liberal nomination. A silence fell over all of us but especially the Layton family. It was a bruising dose of realpolitik, and the moment both Jack and his dad quit the Liberal Party for good and their political paths diverged.

Watching Jack Blossom
MEL WATKINS

One of the joys of professorhood is the students you meet, some of whom become part of your life.

I first met Jack Layton in the 1970s when he was doing graduate work in political science at York University and I was teaching political economy at the University of Toronto. He was writing a doctoral thesis on foreign ownership and the Foreign Investment Review Agency. These being specialties of mine, he came round to consult. He finished his thesis in his matter-of-fact way, and I was asked to be on the committee that examined him orally on it. Years later, Jack would insist to me and to others that I had given him a hard time, but the only recollection I have, which is quite touching, is that the moment we finished examining him and told him he had passed, he excused himself to go to another room and phoned his father.

We both lived in the area around the University of Toronto, and his daughter Sarah and my daughter Emily went to the same school, so we sometimes ran into each other. (In one of life's lovely coincidences, Emily ended up working for the NDP on Parliament Hill, most recently as director of leader affairs in Jack's office.) Over the years Jack had a considerable U of T connection. He was involved for a number of years in the environmental program at Innis College and gave an annual Innis Memorial Lecture. In later years, when our paths crossed, Jack and I talked of the joys of grandparenting.

Jack ran for City Council in the ward in which I lived, and I worked on his campaigns. I particularly remember when he ran for mayor and I was canvassing with him late in the campaign. It was clear that Jack was not doing well, even in his own ward, but he ran up and down the stairs in the low-rises, full of good cheer. It was not the false cheer that I suppose politicians in particular have to learn. It was just the way Jack was, and we now know what an enormous strength it was. Years later, when Jack ran federally, I sometimes canvassed with him at subway stations in the morning rush to work. It's not a time when I'm at my best, but it was truly a pleasure to bounce out of bed and help Jack wish the world good morning.

Opportunities to Serve
RICHARD ZAJCHOWSKI

It was a hot summer evening in 2010. I was visiting Toronto, and Jack and I arranged to meet for a late supper at a pub. Jack arrived; we hugged.

I had a question that had been bothering me for a while, so early in the meal I asked him, "Jack, I was wondering if you felt the same way I did about our early days in Hudson.

We were given so much: loving parents, a wonderful education, a village that was so supportive—we got all the breaks. So I've always felt I had a duty to give back. You know the saying, 'To those whom much is given, much is expected.' Is that what drives you too?" Knowing Jack very well, I was sure he would agree with me.

But Jack surprised me: "Oh no, Zack! That's not what drives me at all. It's the opportunity to serve." Then he explained to me how his dad had inculcated "the opportunity to serve" in all the Layton children. When they were kids, say they would be sitting around the dining-room table after supper. Mr. Layton would say, "Look at all these dirty dishes—here's an opportunity to serve." Now kids are pretty smart, and they would groan at this obvious ploy, but eventually one of them would get up, take the dishes to the kitchen, and start washing. Mr. Layton would then come into the kitchen and start singing and talk with the volunteer about their day. As a result of this encouragement, Jack said, the "opportunity to serve" got woven into his DNA. He was always excited about any opportunity to serve.

Combining Principle and Pleasure
MYER SIEMIATYCKI

Can you imagine Jack Layton as a "twenty-something"?

The trademark qualities that Canadians came to associate with the "sixty-something" Layton when he led his final, heroically inspirational election campaign of 2011 were boundless energy, optimism, and compassion. What words then could capture the persona and presence of a more youthful Layton, at an age when character traits are typically even more intensely manifest?

I had the great fortune of working alongside Jack from 1978 to 1980. (Of course he was ever first-name-bonded to all who held him dear, whether lifelong friends or public admirers.) The Jack Layton I befriended back then was quite simply extraordinary and it was plain for all to see that Jack would make his mark on the world around him.

Jack hired me in 1978. He was then a tenured professor of politics at Ryerson. He had signed on for secondment to deliver a university course on city politics for Open College/ CJRT-FM, Ryerson's distance-education broadcast arm. This entailed preparing forty-eight hours of radio programming that combined lectures and expert-interview clips. Luckily for me, it was regarded as a two-person job, and I was hired to be Jack's partner. Ever since, in his warm, affectionate way, Jack would refer to me as "pardner."

But getting that course on air was never a fully equal partnership—Jack pulled his weight and also some of mine. As he was far more steeped in the subject than I was, Jack generously took on more than a half share of course preparation. For two years we worked side by side in a shared office, days often turning into nights, to get programs on air with the magical studio wizardry of our producer, John Valenteyn.

Jack was a gifted, inspiring teacher. He regarded learning as a pathway to empowerment, helping students to understand their world and what they could do to better it. Before the concept of teaching charrettes became fashionable, Jack focused classes on solving real-world challenges. For many Ryerson students—as their messages following Jack's passing reminded me—the city walking tours on which Jack would lead his classes were the highlight of their university years. Jack taught students how to "read" a city by its sightlines: how power and poverty, advantage and deprivation played out on urban landscapes apparent for all to see. Most fundamentally, Jack taught students that their city could be a better place, and they had an important role to play in making it so.

Conversation was a constant in the office we shared in the late seventies. Jack spoke proudly of having been elected to the post of prime minister in a youth parliament, and it was clear he saw this as more of a dress rehearsal than a fantasy fill-in for the real deal on the Hill. But Jack was most impassioned reflecting on times in his youth when he led the charge to overcome discrimination and injustice around him. There was the time he made sure French teens in his hometown of Hudson could get into the exclusive local yacht club even if they weren't members; again, when he broke down the colour barrier to admission at his university fraternity.

For Jack, politics was played out all around you in everyday life. And it had to measure up to a moral standard of caring, fairness, and equality. It took courage to be a first voice naming injustices. In the years I first knew Jack, his was an often lonely voice in Toronto decrying a host of scourges including environmental degradation, homophobia, poverty, sexism, homelessness, and racism. How many great political leaders do we have who stayed true to those principles their entire lives?

What made Jack all the more endearing was that he was no ascetic. I have never known anyone who had a more robust appetite for life. "Twenty-something" Jack was a whirlwind of ideas and motion, charismatically packaged into an athletic physique, framed by strongly etched face, handlebar moustache, and dark wavy hair. And then there was Jack's way with words. Even then he had a way of naming injustice, making it a mark of shame on all who tolerated its continuation. Jack's emphasis was never to blame but to call people to a higher purpose or values. To remind us that we, and our society, could do better.

Jack soaked up life with great gusto. Amidst all the programming work we did back then, there were endless meetings strategizing to promote the election of more progressive candidates into municipal government. A bar rather than a church basement was the typical meeting place. Invariably the heartiest laugh of the night erupted over a self-deprecating crack Jack would make at his own expense.

Jack knew how to combine principle and pleasure. For example, he loved golf, but not the excessive reliance on chemicals that gave golf courses their manicured look. What was an eco-golfer to do? Leave it to Jack. One gorgeous summer day Jack, fellow Toronto city councillor Joe Mihevc, my son Matti, and I went golfing at a municipal course in Toronto. As we completed the front nine (with Jack shooting the best round), he announced that the rest of us should play ahead; he would meet up with us in a few holes. Asking where he had disappeared to when he turned up several holes later, Jack informed us he had arranged to meet a TV news crew to give an interview on eco-friendly ways of maintaining golf courses. The good things in life—yacht clubs, fraternities, golf courses—were not to be forsaken; they were to be made sustainable and available to all. And every opportunity should be taken to get out the message.

Jack loved music, the more soulful the better. One of my fondest memories of Jack was the road trip we took in 1979 to Quebec City to attend the annual conference of the Federation of Canadian Municipalities (FCM) to record interviews with leading municipal officials for our radio course. (Years later, Jack would be elected president of the FCM.) We loaded the car up with cassettes for the ride—Jack favoured Jimi

Hendrix, and I brought along Van Morrison. From the first notes, Jack became hooked on Morrison's *Moondance* album. It is a distinct delight to recall Jack's thick eyebrows dancing joyfully above his broad smile to the rhythm of Van Morrison. The sounds of Morrison's "Into the Mystic" performed as part of the processional at Jack's funeral were crushingly sad and beautiful.

I was honoured to read an invocation at Jack's funeral. In classic inclusive spirit, the ceremony began with four citations from Aboriginal, Christian, Jewish, and Muslim traditions. As I strode onto the stage approaching the lectern, I couldn't help saying to myself, "Jack, this is our final broadcast together." And as I read the final lines of my selection from the prophet Isaiah, I was reminded how high Jack had set the bar for himself, and how much higher he had soared:

> *If you banish oppression from your midst,*
> *The menacing hand and tainted speech,*
> *If you give of yourself to the hungry,*
> *Fulfilling the needs of the poor—*
> *Then shall your light shine in darkness,*
> *And your darkness shall be like the noon.*
> *Then shall you be like a garden given water,*
> *Like a wellspring whose waters never fail.*
> *And you shall lay foundations for the coming*
> *generation.*

A Mentor Mentored
DAVID V. J. BELL

Jack Layton was my friend. He was also one of my graduate students, and I supervised his doctoral dissertation at York University, where he earned his PhD in Political Science in 1983 with a dissertation entitled "Capital and the Canadian State: Foreign Investment Policy 1957–1983." By that time Jack was well beyond the allowable time limit for completing the degree, which he had started ten years earlier! Jack had completed all his coursework and other requirements in a timely fashion and had been ABD (All But Dissertation) for nearly six years. During that period he had secured a full-time teaching position in the politics department at Ryerson and had begun his foray into municipal politics.

I had pretty much given up hope that Jack would ever complete the degree, so I was very surprised when he contacted me in early 1983 to let me know that he had finished a draft of his dissertation. But there was a problem. By the early 1980s all graduate programs in the province were under the gun to reduce doctoral students' permissible times to completion. York's new dean of graduate studies had adopted the rather draconian policy of requiring any PhD student beyond his or her time limit seeking to re-enrol to complete the degree to obtain a letter of permission from the dean! The request to the dean for permission to re-enrol had to come directly from the supervisor, writing on the student's behalf.

In the front of his personal copy of his dissertation, Jack kept two letters—the first was the letter from his supervisor to the dean, pleading the case that Jack Layton should be allowed to re-enrol in the political science doctoral program to complete his degree. The second letter, written and signed the same day, was from the dean acknowledging the special circumstances that had contributed to Mr. Layton's delay in completing the final requirement for the degree and granting permission for him to re-enrol. Jack kept these two letters because he loved their symmetry: I was both his supervisor and the dean of graduate studies, so I had authored and signed both letters. I had to write to myself extolling the merits of the candidate and then write back to myself accepting the compelling logic of my argument.

Jack often referred to me as his "old professor." He was not referring to my advanced years—the age difference between us was only six years. We played squash together while he was doing his coursework at York. We also made music together at my annual party for my graduate students. Jack played guitar, sang, and played piano. He loved to laugh and have fun, and was often the life of the party.

Jack told others that he counted me as one of his mentors, but I'm sure I learned at least as much from him as he did from me. This is just further confirmation of the motto *docendo discimus*—we learn by teaching. I learned plenty from Jack about an area I came to "profess" after I switched my academic appointment from political science to the Faculty of Environmental Studies (FES), where I was appointed dean in 1992.

While I was becoming more familiar with theories and ideas related to environment and sustainability in FES, Jack got hands-on experience in the practical world of environmental enterprise. After his unsuccessful bid to become mayor of Toronto in 1991, Jack founded an environmental consulting business called the Green Catalyst Group Inc. Jack became an articulate, well-informed champion of many environmental causes and brought his passion with him on his re-election to municipal office as a Metro councillor in 1994.

In this, his second incarnation as a local politician, Jack reshaped his image and changed his approach. He sometimes said that he went from "opposing" to "proposing," and one of the things he proposed to the newly elected mayor of the amalgamated City of Toronto, Mel Lastman, was the establishment of an Environmental Task Force (ETF). This was a brilliant stroke on Jack's part. The forced amalgamation of what had been seven separate municipal entities created a conundrum regarding environmental policies and practices: which of the seven jurisdictional approaches would be adopted for the new entity? Or was there an opportunity for raising the bar and improving environmental performance overall?

The ETF brought together a broad range of stakeholders including city politicians and senior officials, representatives of other levels of government and relevant agencies such as the Toronto and Region Conservation Authority, environmental NGOs, private-sector representatives from both business and labour, a few academics, and concerned citizens. It was an excellent process of mutual learning. We had strong staff support, but the overall guidance and leadership came from Jack. His presence in the room lifted morale and raised the level of discussion. Although he urged us to "take a fifty-year lens" to the topics and issues we dealt with, he also insisted that we look for "quick starts" and positive outcomes that could be achieved in the short term. These accomplishments were reported at the beginning of every meeting and helped sustain the group's commitment and enthusiasm.

In April 2000 the ETF produced an excellent report,

Clean, Green and Healthy: A Plan for an Environmentally Sustainable Toronto. It contained many useful recommendations for the city with regard to land, water, air, sustainable transportation, sustainable energy use, green economic development, education and awareness, governance, and measuring and reporting progress. Moreover, working with the ETF staff, Toronto hosted an important conference on sustainability indicators that resulted in the formation of CSIN (Canadian Sustainability Indicators Network)—a wonderful legacy for the many sustainability professionals across the country. The ETF's report included a recommendation to establish a Toronto Sustainability Roundtable (SRT), which continued and extended its work for the next four years. Again Jack was the architect of its success.

Around the same time, Jack was gaining a high profile in the Federation of Canadian Municipalities (FCM), and he soon rose to the position of president. This gave him a platform from which to advance the cause of municipal sustainability across the country. He was a key figure in the successful negotiation with the federal government that allowed large cities a share of the gas tax and the arrangement to provide infrastructure funding to municipalities on the condition that they first produce a sustainability action plan. His work as president of the FCM took Jack to all parts of Canada and inspired him to shift his focus to the national political stage.

With Jack's death on August 22, 2011, Canada lost not only a strong political leader but also the country's most important sustainability champion. In his stirring eulogy at Jack Layton's state funeral, Stephen Lewis, former leader of the Ontario New Democratic Party, described Jack's remarkable letter to Canadians, written just hours before his death, as a "manifesto of social democracy." I saw it somewhat differently, as an outline of Jack Layton's vision of a sustainable future for Canada. Jack understood implicitly and comprehensively that sustainability requires a new politics of inclusiveness rooted in social justice, a sustainable economy, and concern for the environment. All three of these key dimensions of sustainability feature in the letter, and also in the message Jack delivered so eloquently in his final press conference, at which he announced the "new form of cancer" that would claim his life within a few short weeks.

Great leaders, to paraphrase George Bernard Shaw, not only see the world as it is and ask why; they can see a world that has never been and ask why not. Jack was such a leader. He was positive, encouraging, and optimistic. He made others feel energized and hopeful. I sorely miss his friendship but his vision will continue to inspire me and countless others forever.

Each Verse a Universe
E. T. JACKSON

When I think of Jack Layton, I think of a sky full of stars.

Writing half a century ago, Quebec-based jurist-poet and CCF co-founder Frank Scott understood that human beings live their lives in patterns that are microcosms of the universe and its enduring laws. "Each verse/a universe," wrote Scott. Equality and stewardship, service and love—these were the principles that shaped Jack Layton's very public life.

I met Jack directly only twice. I don't want to make too much of these encounters, but for me they were significant. He was a strong and intelligent force of nature, and if you weren't affected by your interaction with him, you were simply not alert to the wonders of life.

The first time I met Jack was at a state dinner for the prime minister of Vietnam, held at the National Gallery in Ottawa on a warm evening in late June 2005. Paul Martin, the prime minister of the day, escorted the guest of honour up the long hallway and into the great glass rotunda. Dignified and calm, Jack followed alone behind the official party, eventually sitting at a table in the audience like the rest of us—though, unlike the rest of us, he received a nod of welcome directly from Mr. Martin.

During the speeches, I occasionally looked over at Jack: his curiosity, intellect, and civility were evident at all times, as was his sense of humour, his joie de vivre. The head table speeches were boilerplate, but Vietnam is such a fascinating, complex, and promising country that the whole event triggered stimulating discussions at every table. Noisy, positive energy filled the big room, and Jack was in the middle of it, loving it all.

Later, as I was leaving, I saw Jack striding towards the door and held it open for him. "How did you like it?" he asked. Somewhat taken aback, I said, unimaginatively, "Vietnam's an important country." "You're right," said Jack, immediately making me feel comfortable (and a bit like a genius pundit). We walked towards the Château Laurier, quickly immersed in a real conversation about the need for Canada to expand trade in southeast Asia, a region he clearly, and not surprisingly, knew a lot about. Much too soon for me, he said good night. I watched him, still fit and energetic at midnight, cross the street under a canopy of bright stars. They shone. And he shone.

My second interaction with Jack was at a leader's

roundtable on economic policy, held in the West Block on Parliament Hill in mid-July 2009. Along with twenty other academics, union staffers, and politicians, I had been invited by his senior policy advisor, Peter Puxley, to present my ideas on business and employment creation. Participants included Ed Broadbent, Olivia Chow, and Peggy Nash, all of whom had very smart things to say. Jack presided, listening intently, asking pointed questions, and showing not only that he'd been thinking a lot about these matters but also that he was already two or three steps ahead of us. Gracious, welcoming, serious, Jack had clearly grown as a national leader.

He now had political and intellectual momentum, and he signalled to every roundtable member that he wanted their best stuff, their most thoughtful, actionable policy recommendations. The world was, haltingly, just coming out of the 2008 debt crisis, and economic policy was a high-stakes enterprise, as it still is. We all tried hard to make our contributions succinct and practical, and Jack kept the conversation moving forward, crisp and efficient, continuously connecting people and ideas.

When it was all over, he thanked everyone personally. We hugged. He had been working out, and so, fortunately, had I; it was probably one of the more forceful social-democratic embraces that summer, and we were both delighted. You could build an NDP-Liberal coalition around a hug like that, I thought as I left the building, and I later blogged about what such a coalition would look like and might actually do.

I also thought of a sky full of stars. Jack Layton had shone again—in fact, he had been *luminous*—from the beginning of the session until its very last moment. He had put it all together: energy, wit, focus, good cheer, vision, and, well, *wisdom*. We all wanted to work with him to build a better

Canada. On that day, in that room in the West Block, it was clear to all of us that Jack would make a fine prime minister. It would later become evident to millions of other Canadians.

Sky full of stars. Each verse a universe.

Learning from Your Hero
SVEND ROBINSON

Noam Chomsky was a hero, an icon for Jack. He told me several times that Noam's book *Hegemony or Survival* was the most profound work that he had read, and that he found it deeply inspiring both politically and personally. For that reason I was very excited when Noam agreed to be the keynote speaker at a celebration in Vancouver of my twenty-five years in Parliament in March 2004. This was the first and only time that Noam had agreed to speak at such an event for a national politician, and I was deeply honoured. We had worked together on a number of issues over the years, including East Timor and the Palestinian question. Noam also agreed to speak at an anti-Iraq War rally while in Vancouver on that day.

Jack was thrilled and immediately asked if I could arrange for a meeting with Noam when he came to Vancouver for the celebration. At that point Jack had been leader of the federal NDP for a little over a year, but was not yet elected to the House. Noam agreed without hesitation.

Together with Jack, my partner Max and I met with Noam for breakfast at his hotel. Jack was almost like a little boy meeting his idol, telling me that this was something he had hoped for over the course of many years. During the breakfast, Jack and Noam had a terrific conversation and developed a strong bond. Noam told me afterwards how impressed he was with Jack, and how absolutely impossible it would have been for Jack to attain a leadership position (or me to ever be elected!) in the US political culture in which big corporate money had such influence. They agreed to stay in contact and did communicate a number of times in subsequent years.

Later that glorious sunny day, both Jack and Noam spoke passionately to thousands of antiwar protesters in Vancouver's West End. That evening, they joined a sold-out crowd at the Orpheum theatre at my twenty-fifth anniversary celebration, and my Burnaby riding executive presented both with exquisite carved Haida talking sticks. At the end of the day Jack gave me a big hug; with tears in his eyes, he said it had been one of the best days of his life and repeated what a thrill it was for him to have been able to spend the day with Noam.

Two years later, in early 2006, Jack sent Noam an invitation to be the keynote speaker at the upcoming NDP federal convention in Quebec City. In an email, he wrote, "With our new minority government with a right-wing Prime Minister, your analysis and vision forward is more important than ever. Thanks for your latest book on failed states!" Sadly, Noam was unable to come to the convention, but which other political leader in Canada would have had the courage and vision to invite Noam Chomsky to address his party's national convention, knowing full well the storm of controversy and attacks that invitation would invite? Only Jack.

I received a brief, heartfelt message from Noam Chomsky shortly after Jack's death. He mourned this tragic loss of a great man and, like me, dared to think about what might have been, how our country and our world would have been changed by the election of Prime Minister Jack Layton.

Jack, with cousins Diane and Barbara McIntyre, at the Layton summer home in Knowlton, 1952.

Thirteen members of the extended Layton family in Knowlton, circa 1961. Jack is in the centre of the photo, with his hand resting on the shoulder of his younger brother, Rob.

Jack was a serious Canadian swimming champion, competing on the McGill Water Polo Team while at university. He is fourteen in this shot.

Jack (centre) with other junior members of the Hudson Yacht Club, circa 1962.

JACK LAYTON
"A man is not what he thinks he is, but what he thinks, he is!" Jack is the most exteemed president of our Student's Council and also the supporter of all school activities. He always wears a bright smile which displays his natural friendliness to the world. In the past year he has proven

Page 26

Jack in his high school yearbook, circa 1966.

Courtesy of Rod Hodgson

Jack as an auctioneer, circa 1986.

Courtesy of Debbie Field

Jack, standing beside his bicycle in 1986, when he was a Toronto city councillor.

2

The Heart of the City

After years of teaching students about the relationship between values and politics, Jack was ready to put himself in the thick of political action. And where better to start than in Toronto, a large city where many of its politicians still acted and thought as though it were a small town? There was lots of work to be done.

Jack was first elected as a Toronto alderman in 1982 and then as councillor in 1985, after the amalgamation of Metropolitan Toronto. It didn't take long for his vision—and his cockiness—to polarize City Council. For Jack, the job was much bigger than simply working for or against particular motions and ideas raised in the council chamber. The city was the people in it, the communities they built, and the environments they lived in.

Some of his ideas were hugely unpopular. His opposition

to the random development of downtown and waterfront land, to the city's 1996 Olympic bid, and to funding of the SkyDome sports arena certainly made him some enemies. Other ideas were simply too prescient for the Council to understand at first, such as the need for the city to fund AIDS education.

But for Jack, everything could be made better and everything had political potential. No matter how determined, condescending, or downright rude the opposition to his practical ideas might be—sometimes the old guard just laughed—he, and like-minded councillors, kept at it. During his time on Council, he chaired virtually all the committees and task forces grappling with the issues close to his heart —health, economic development, transportation, homelessness, the environment, cycling, and renewable energy. His tactics never changed: he stuck to the issues, never made it personal, often charmed even those who disagreed with him—and won often enough, and amiably enough, to help to bring a new vision to Toronto.

During his term as president of the Federation of Canadian Municipalities, Jack brought his issues to other Canadian cities as well. As busy as he was during this period, he still found the time to write a book about a subject that was vital to him. Entitled *Homelessness: The Making and Unmaking of a Crisis*, his book was hailed as an important study.

The Downtowner
KEVIN SYLVESTER

Everyone talks about Jack Layton's moustache. It's a different feature that pops into my head when I hear Jack's name.

I remember him wearing a bike helmet.

Jack was a perfect downtowner. He never drove if he could bike or walk. (He even dumped his full-time car when he was on City Council.) You'd see a crowd waving to some guy peddling through Kensington or near Christie Pits, and then see Jack wave back or ring his bell.

He'd appear at mass rides, rallies for fallen cyclists. He'd helped set up the first Toronto cycling committee and was one of the designers of the ring-and-post bike posts. Jack famously campaigned on a bike. He rode in the gay pride parade—often on a tandem bike with his wife Olivia. He rode to City Council meetings, and rode in all kinds of weather.

One of my proudest moments working at CBC Radio was a simple nod from Jack, not about my sports reporting but about my cycling reports. (Andy Barrie, the host of *Metro Morning* when I did sports, had been tickled by my insistence on commuting on a bike all year long. He'd ask me to rate the winter weather by how many of my fingers had gone numb on the ride to work.) One day Jack was coming in for an interview and was standing outside the studio door when I finished my sports report. I held the door and he paused.

"Nice cycling. Keep up the good work," he said, before heading inside.

I still smile at the memory. Not because someone famous had recognized me (although that's always nice), and not because I shared his politics. (As editor of the newspaper at St. Michael's College in the University of Toronto, I once wrote a screed against Jack when he'd helped scuttle a proposal to build a condo on the property—St. Mike's needed that cash.) The reason I smile is that Jack had incredible cred, and he had listened and approved of what I was doing.

Jack wearing a helmet is a symbol of how to live in a city. It reflects how our leaders view where they live and the people who live alongside them.

Drive your car through a city and you see five interesting things, if you're lucky. Ride your bike and you see a thousand. In a car you see a group of people. On a bike you see a family sharing a story, holding hands, laughing.

Never trust a politician who drives to the grocery store.

Politics in Love
JOE MIHEVC

It is impossible to speak about Jack's life and work without bringing in Olivia. Jack and Olivia were not just personal partners. They were political soulmates in a most profound way. Sitting between them in council chambers, I would sometimes catch their eye movements communicating with each other. Jack's principal strategist in gaining the leadership of the NDP was Olivia, who could give a province-by-province analysis of the leadership campaign in precise detail followed by a clear strategy of the next steps required. Olivia could match his energy and commitment like no one else. They were clearly of one mind, which made them a powerful political force on City Council far beyond the two votes that they commanded. Politics did not strain their relationship the way it does for many a couple; in their case, politics enriched them as a couple and nurtured their love for each other.

Let the Games Begin
ADAM VAUGHAN

Over the course of our careers Jack and I found time to work together, argue with each other, and fight or do battle in too many elections to count. Most of our relationship was played out with me as a reporter and Jack as a politician in Toronto. But whether we were allies or rivals or just sharing a beer, I hope we had the most common ground when we found a way to laugh at it all and, perhaps most important, to chuckle at ourselves along the way.

One of my fondest memories of just such an event involved a collaborative effort that went absolutely nowhere.

It began just after Jack had written his book on the housing crisis and I had just completed a series of news stories on Toronto's Tent City, a shantytown that had sprung up on Toronto's waterfront while Jack was a councillor and I was a reporter for Citytv. The city was in the throes of mounting another Olympic bid and Tent City just happened to be located at the gateway to the land where the athletes' village and the main stadiums would be located. The campaign for public housing was in full swing, and Tent City symbolized both the failure of government and the promise of what might be solved by winning the games for Toronto.

A prominent player in the Toronto film industry approached Jack and me about the possibility of doing some sort of docudrama about homelessness, with Tent City as a storyline. It was all very serious: statistics, the drama of the housing crisis, a renegade group of activists, and a colourful band of homeless folks, complete with government clashes, the police, and the courts—all set against the backdrop of a global city. Jack and I were hired as experts, and after an initial couple of meetings we decided that we were ready for Hollywood. What could go wrong? "Lights, camera, action!" we proudly proclaimed.

Action? Perhaps inaction would have been a better word for it.

The project was going nowhere and, in fact, went nowhere for lots of good reasons, but one night over beers in Jack's backyard as we realized our star would never shine in Hollywood a new proposal was hatched—and this one went nowhere even faster. We decided to drop the whole documentary component of the project and with it our big-time film partner. Our commitment to fight for a national housing policy still burned brightly, however. Something had to be done.

Facts and figures weren't winning the fight to end homelessness, and activist fatigue was setting in on the issue. A slew of very serious reports and books and government programs and campaigns had all been launched. Yet somehow, the very simple solution—just build more public housing—seemed just beyond everyone's grasp. Instead, that night, we constructed a proposal for a very different motion picture. We decided to script a feature film. Screw reality. Go big or go home, we agreed, and it was at this point that politics left the table and the beer began talking. To our own screams of laughter we concocted a plot that spun right out of control.

Tent City would still set the scene; the backdrop would still be a shantytown of homemade houses, tents, and abandoned caravans circled around a set of wintery campfires on the shores of Lake Ontario—all that was fine. The film would still have activists, experts, and politicians, but they would merely be background characters. In this project the homeless who actually lived in Toronto's Tent City would work on the film; Jack even insisted that they star as themselves. This wasn't to be just about Toronto: Jack and I were hatching a plot on behalf of street folk everywhere.

Unlike what happened in real life, Toronto would win its bid to host the Olympics in our movie. From there the plot evolved with a drunken mix of glee and paranoia: the games were coming, and with them the multinational fast-food restaurants, the running-shoe companies, the hotel developers. The jet set was about to descend on Toronto's Tent City, with the world's media and political elite in tow. The International Olympic Committee wanted everything to go according to plan, and so did City Hall. For the rich to play, the poor must be booted from their lakeside home. The police would order the eviction of Tent City; the land was to be cleared and sold. The homeless, with their scavenged computers, old TVs, and stolen electricity, caught wind of the conspiracy and began to plot their last stand.

A wise old maritimer, with a love of rum and poetry (in that order), would watch as the zealots and newly arrived radicals and drifters plotted and schemed to defend the shantytown. An armed confrontation was inevitable. The old-timer was sceptical; he was just about to pack up and leave when he had an epiphanic vision: a new Tent City must rise on this land—a new United Nations for the poor, with the clarion call of "housing for all!" I'm still not sure if Jack didn't have ideas about casting himself as the first secretary-general!

Ah, but for this cinematic utopia to rise on the shores of Lake Ontario the Olympics would have to be stopped. In one version of our script that night, the vision to lead the insurrection was delivered to the old-timer by the ghost of Emma Goldman. That was my idea. Jack, true to his NDP roots, argued for Tommy Douglas. I'm not sure we ever resolved that point.

At some time during this mad attempt at scriptwriting (neither of us actually had pen or paper), a bottle of rum was added to the mix of beer and bluster, and that's when Jack and I really got carried away. The movie's pace quickened. The old-timer would steal a boat from a nearby yacht club and sail across the lake to the United States. The plan was obvious: in the States there were guns and homeless war vets aplenty, and armed and trained troops were needed. A smuggling ring would be formed and the number of weapons and rebels would grow. Tent City would have to develop suburbs, kids would be born, a church started, and a city hall formed. I argued for a pirate radio station. At some point I think we reminded ourselves that this was only going to be a movie; as the story was reaching a climax, clouds gathered on the horizon. The shantytown had taken on Olympian proportions. But while all this was happening the forces of evil were coming down to the lake ready to evict, and things were about to get nasty.

For Jack it was all a classic tale of how the West was won, with a bit of class warfare thrown in for good measure. The plot twists and the instant creation of new characters, each modelled on a friend or a foe, were liberating—Jack and I were clearly working out a few frustrations. We agreed this wouldn't just be a movie, but an allegory for our times, a brilliant satire, a political drama in which every outcome and retribution would serve a vision of true social justice.

It would be an epic!

The movie would end in a Sam Peckinpah-inspired hail of sound and fury. Bullets would fly as fast and as furiously as the beer bottles were flying out of Jack's beer fridge. Tent City and its mythical inhabitants would refuse to budge; the homeless would stand their ground and defeat the multinational forces wanting to evict them. The Olympics would never come to town and Tent City would become the shining city on the shore, a beacon for all those seeking truth, justice, and the Canadian way.

Did I mention it was to be an epic?

Of course, it had to have a happy ending. It was to be a classic Layton finish: love triumphed over hate, optimism trumped despair, and the world was changed for the better. True, we never made the movie—but it was a hell of a good night and an awfully fun story.

Cue the Music
RICHARD BARRY

From 1992 to 2003 it would have been an unusual week that Jack Layton and I weren't working together on one project or another. For me, it started with his first run for federal Parliament in Rosedale. Then in 1994 I began a five-year stint as executive director of the White Ribbon Campaign on violence against women. Jack was the co-chair of the board and we worked very closely to build the organization. In 1999, I went to work in his City Hall office and was his executive assistant for his term as president of the Federation of Canadian Municipalities. Along the way there were always various election campaigns to work on or to manage and, of course, the NDP leadership campaign. By the time he headed to Ottawa in the winter of 2003 and I turned my attention to my partner MPP Marilyn Churley's re-election campaign that fall, he and I had logged some serious mileage together.

Of all the things I could mention about Jack as I knew

him, one of the most interesting was his love of music. It's something we shared and something we tried to weave into almost everything we did together.

Anyone who ever attended a party at Jack and Olivia's house knew that, as the night wore on, copies of the Pete Seeger singalong book *Rise Up Singing* would be passed around. Page numbers would be called out for favourite songs and everyone would join in. Jack was always in the middle of the fun, playing some very serviceable guitar on an old twelve-string he had for many years. As most people know, Jack loved to play the piano, and it would frequently happen that we would end our music nights with his special version of "Hit the Road, Jack." He used to joke that it wasn't the best song for a politician to sing, but it was a song he really enjoyed.

One of my favourite stories involves the 2004 federal campaign. Jack was on the campaign plane leading the press contingent in song, as he frequently did. I was in Ottawa working in the war room when my phone rang. It was Jack, with a lot of noise and much gaiety in the background, asking me how many of the words to Stan Rogers's "Barrett's Privateers" I could remember. With his cellphone to his head and guitar in hand, he sang as I fed him as many lines as I could recall.

In 1993, Jack and I were upstairs at a bar on Church Street when the Blue Jays beat Philadelphia to win their second World Series title. We were sitting at the bar, shoulder to shoulder, when Joe Carter's home run sailed over the left-field fence to seal the victory. Things went a little crazy from there. Jack knew he had to do something special to celebrate, so he ran home and got his Selmer Super Action 80 alto saxophone, then hit the streets to make some noise among all the partiers. Now Jack would have been the first to tell you that he never really learned to play the saxophone. But he could squeak out

a handful of notes. I think he could almost do a recognizable version of "Na Na Hey Hey (Kiss Him Goodbye)." No
matter, he was having a blast and we partied the night away
on lower Yonge Street. When I finally went home, Jack was
still standing in a bank building alcove playing his heart out.
I'm proud to say that I have that alto saxophone and put it to
some good use, if I do say so myself.

In 2001, Jack ran for the presidency of the Federation of
Canadian Municipalities at a convention in London, Ontario.
He wanted to drum up some excitement for our campaign, so
on the night of the biggest party at the convention, Jack and I
strapped on our guitars and marched into the room singing as
loudly as we could. I can't remember what we sang, but everyone loved it, and he sailed to victory on the convention floor
the next day (not that the two events were necessary related).

There are lots more stories about local musicians joining
us for various fundraisers and other events, busking together
on the Danforth in Toronto just a couple of years ago as part
of a Stephen Lewis Foundation fundraiser, or Jack at the
piano in our living room at the party we had when Marilyn
and I got married. Jack tried to make music a part of so much
he did. In the tradition of Pete Seeger, Woody Guthrie, Billy
Bragg, and so many others, he always understood the power
of song. But mostly, Jack just loved the music.

Pitching In
ANNE GOLDEN

All Canadians, regardless of political views, had tremendous
respect and affection for Jack. We admired his charisma, his
intelligence, his dedication to the causes he believed in, his

devotion to his family, and his passion for making life better for all Canadians. I had the opportunity to get to know Jack through several decades. We first worked together on municipal issues in the 1970s when he was at Ryerson and I was at the Bureau of Municipal Research.

The quality that I found most endearing was his personal generosity when the cameras were off and when there was no possible political or personal gain. When I was planning a conference on the role of the media in municipal issues, it was Jack who helped me by filming the three-day City Hall debate on the fifty-five-foot height bylaw. When I was at the United Way of Greater Toronto, Jack was always ready to help in any way he could in the United Way campaign, no matter how busy he was at City Hall. We worked closely on homelessness: he spent considerable time with my taskforce helping us to understand the issues in detail, even leading us on an evening tour.

Jack was always so generous with his personal time to help the community. It is so sad that we have lost an extraordinary Canadian with so much more to give, though he gave us all so much.

On the Streets
CATHY CROWE

Late 1980s. It was likely a typical Saturday morning for Jack, cycling to what would have been the first in a series of community events. On this particular Saturday his first stop was a public "Inquiry into Health and Homelessness," held at a downtown community centre. As I tried to squeeze into the packed room of mostly homeless and low-income people, I heard a young Jack Layton, Toronto city councillor and Board of Health chair, speaking. His passion for this issue was matched only by his outrage and his determination to do something about it.

I already knew Jack, but this inquiry, along with Jack's rallying call for justice, inspired a turn in my career. I became a "street nurse," working on the "downstream" end results of homelessness—infections (such as tuberculosis), trauma, and death—and also trying to propose solutions to prevent homelessness, such as building housing.

While I was doing the nursing piece, Jack used his considerable skills at City and Metro halls to push the issue to the political forefront. Our paths frequently crossed— often, I'm sad to say, in tragedy, but that made the victories we did have all the sweeter.

A politically savvy city councillor, Jack literally worked with his sleeves rolled up, whether he was chairing the incredibly democratic Homeless Advisory Committee at City Hall, which he convinced Mayor Mel Lastman to allow him to create, or working with us out on the street, where conditions were worsening daily.

I don't think Jack ever got over the first cluster of homeless freezing deaths in Toronto. He wrote and spoke about it repeatedly over the years. It was 1996, and one of the three men who froze to death on a winter night was Eugene Upper, who died on Spadina Avenue—walking distance, as Jack pointed out, from his and Olivia's home. This death galvanized Jack into action, seeking emergency city funding for street-outreach agencies, supporting activists' call for the subsequent inquest, and leading the public-policy follow-up to push all three levels of government to implement the jury recommendations. One of the more practical recommendations was the implementation of Toronto's cold weather alert system. Jack likely believed and hoped, as I did, that all would be well.

Then one bright sunny Sunday in January, a year after the freezing deaths, the *Toronto Sun* called to inform me that a homeless man named Garland Sheppard had frozen to death overnight. Did I have a comment? I was stunned and couldn't comment, but I did get more details from the journalist. I learned that the previous night's temperature had been -17 degrees Celsius with the wind chill at -30 degrees. Shockingly, the city had not implemented its new cold weather alert system, which would have triggered the opening of more shelter beds and increased street outreach by agencies to prevent such a needless death.

Garland Sheppard, known as "Newf" on the street, had been found in the morning "cold to the touch" by a homeless friend who called 911. Paramedics took him to St. Michael's Hospital, where he died. I was overwhelmed with grief, naively having thought that inquest recommendations and new practices would have prevented this tragedy from repeating itself.

Coincidentally, Jack was in my co-op that Sunday chairing a meeting. I entered the meeting room, approached him, and whispered the shocking news. He immediately and solemnly excused himself, and then leapt into action, delineating the steps we would take. Within minutes he was in my apartment, hammering out a press release on my computer and sending it to Olivia to release to the media. Next, we went to the site where Mr. Sheppard had been found. It was an unused third floor of a parking garage in the downtown core. It was a disturbing site, with signs of multiple people sleeping there: clothing, piles of sleeping bags, and personal belongings.

Jack had called a press conference at the site. The media release he hammered out noted, "The body is thawing at St. Michael's Hospital. The precise cause of the man's death awaits a full medical examination once the body is thawed." His next step was to take the issue up again at City Hall, and he embarrassed city officials into immediately implementing the cold weather alert. In the following years Jack continued to make the point, which he noted in that media release, that "sleeping bags and blankets cannot prevent these deaths— hostel beds and permanent housing can."

Sadly, deaths like Sheppard's not only continued but increased. That's why Jack spoke out at the Toronto Homeless Memorial, suggesting that certain government policies had caused these deaths. This created a national media frenzy. I was very surprised at the reaction to his comment, because it was self-evidently true.

As homeless conditions worsened, Jack upped the ante, turning every challenge into an opportunity:

1. *Mel Lastman's 1997 declaration during his mayoralty campaign that there were "no homeless in North York" sharply contrasted with Toronto Disaster Relief Committee's (TDRC) 1998 declaration that homelessness was a national disaster.* No problem: Jack convinced the newly elected mayor to appoint him as Toronto Council's point person on housing and homelessness.

In fact, in his book *Homelessness: The Making and Unmaking of a Crisis*, Jack notes that "before he was sworn in as the mayor of the new mega-city, Lastman told me that he was so deeply shaken by what had happened (the outrage and media fiasco that followed Lastman's no homeless statement) that he was going to make homelessness his top priority—the first problem he would tackle as mayor." Jack reported he had never witnessed such a powerful epiphany in Canadian politics. It was likely due to Jack's savvy staging of events that Lastman hosted his first press conference on the issue in a homeless shelter.

In the meantime, we convinced Jack to take TDRC's disaster declaration to the national level, calling for homelessness relief and the 1 per cent solution—an additional 1 per cent of federal and provincial budgets to be allocated to a national housing program. He took on the challenge and successfully convinced the Big City Mayors' caucus of the Federation of Canadian Municipalities to support the declaration. This was one of the sweet victories, as it catapulted homelessness onto the national agenda and resulted in an entirely new federal homelessness program and more than $1 billion infused into communities across the country.

2. *Years of City Hall bureaucrats denying we had a shelter problem.* No problem: Jack convinced the city's shelter manager and medical officer of health to come on a nighttime tour with him and TDRC, all under the watchful eye of media and a documentary filmmaker. Hundreds of new shelter beds were opened during these years and shelter standards were dramatically improved.

3. *City Hall threatening to evict the Tent City waterfront encampment.* No problem: Jack joined the Tent City leaders and activists and we hiked around the Toronto waterfront at night looking for a relocation site. This is where Jack really shone. I think what he loved most about his job was the ability to remain connected to the grassroots, to the people most affected by issues.

Jack was absolutely stalwart in his support for the people living in Tent City and the youth at Rooster Squat, as he saw their health and sense of self benefit from the disaster relief—the tents, trailers, prefab homes, portable toilets, generators, and woodstoves—that we brought in. He provided a protective shield around that patch of ground, managing the impossible, negotiating with the corporate landowner, Home Depot, and City of Toronto officials to allow Tent City to survive—and it did survive for three years. When that fateful and brutal eviction day finally came, with not even an hour's warning, Jack was there for the final push, helping us to win the historic, pilot rent-supplement program that would provide affordable housing for Tent City residents. We are fortunate that some of Jack's actions are immortalized in Michael Connolly's documentary film *Shelter from the Storm*. They are a lesson in activism, passion, truth-telling, and social justice.

Over the years, whenever I ran into Jack while wearing my 1 per cent button he would ask for it, saying he had given his away to someone else. I always obliged. I'm sure he would appreciate the irony of the Occupy Movement and its articulation of the 1 per cent and the 99 per cent.

In his very last email to me, during my recent provincial election run, Jack encouraged me to keep up the fight, writing, "That riding has been the preserve of the elites for far too long." I discovered for myself that social and economic justice is a very hard fight, but what I learned from Jack is that it's worth the fight and wins are obtainable.

Jack's Training Ground
PAUL J. BEDFORD

Toronto proved to be an excellent training ground for Jack, where he had an opportunity to share his views, test them out on the streets, and engage people of all political stripes to come together to build a better city.

I first encountered Jack in 1982 when I was the director of community and neighbourhoods planning in the city planning department and Jack was a new councillor representing downtown neighbourhoods. I recall walking into his office to discover a beehive of political activity with wall-to-wall desks for numerous assistants and students all working at a fever pitch on both local and citywide issues. Jack clearly loved this kind of work environment and seemed to thrive on the energy of young people who shared his passion for positive change. Every square inch of wall space was covered with maps of all sorts; since I am a passionate urban geographer, that immediately captured my interest. As I talked about his ideas and goals, it became obvious that he was a unique councillor who wanted to make a huge difference in shaping the future of Toronto.

His passions were all-encompassing. They included affordable housing, transit, equity, environment, neighbourhoods, community engagement, urban design, HIV/AIDS, and food security. He recognized the strong connection between good city planning and proactive public health, so he channelled his energy into all these areas through the lens of public health. His deep commitment to addressing the AIDS crisis and to fighting for the underprivileged members of society were at the heart of his work. Above all, he believed in making Toronto a livable city, with equal access to the basics of food, housing, jobs, and education as the fundamental building blocks. But he also knew that a livable city was one that was vital, safe, and healthy.

In his role as chair of the Board of Health from 1985 to 1991, he viewed the city as an urban ecosystem in which all the parts should be seen as interconnected pieces of the same whole. This philosophy led to a landmark report, *Healthy Toronto 2000*, published in 1988. It was way ahead of its time in that it spelled out a clear vision for how Torontonians could come together to find solutions to current problems while embracing ideas for the future. It launched a new way for city departments to work together through the creation of an interdepartmental workgroup of proactive staff who shared a passion for making a difference. It was a creative and positive time that allowed staff to get out of their traditional silo thinking. I was fortunate to be chosen as the head of the workgroup, which led to the formation of a Healthy City Office and the first *State of the City* report, unveiled at the top of the CN Tower. The concept of an annual report card was introduced to measure progress on key issues from year to year and term by term.

This idea has been continued today in the amalgamated City of Toronto by the Toronto Community Foundation's annual *Vital Signs* report, which comes out each fall. This report takes the pulse of the physical, social, economic, community, and environmental health of the city and measures these dimensions against other cities. It has become an excellent means of talking about difficult issues and bringing resources together from all walks of life. As the father of the Healthy City movement and the first *State of the City* report, Jack's pioneering work in the 1980s lives on.

Jack also established the Environmental Protection Office in 1987 in response to growing concerns about the impact of environmental contaminants on human health. He chaired the first Environmental Task Force, which created the first environmental plan for the amalgamated city of Toronto.

In 1987, Jack convinced City Council to approve a $10

million special budget for an AIDS operational plan that included education, case follow-up, and policy development. It resulted in the creation of grants for community groups to develop specific programs.

In 1991, he also played a lead role in establishing the Toronto Food Policy Council, the first such body in North America.

With his interest in the health of fellow Torontonians, it was no surprise that Jack was a champion of personal physical fitness. He was a regular lunchtime participant in the newly established fitness centre in the basement of City Hall and delighted in leading employees in various routines. He was in very good physical shape and had no hesitation in demonstrating his prowess.

I also remember his work to transform the railway lands south of Front Street from what was originally slated to be a major continuation of the commercial-financial district into a downtown residential community where people could walk to work. Jack was also an advocate of locating the SkyDome next to Union Station, making it possible for the stadium to be built with very little parking, given the availability of subway and GO Transit. These lands are now in a ten-year process of being developed into a high-density community with a major new park, school, and community centre in addition to retail support services and office employment.

After the amalgamation of Toronto in 1998, Jack took on new citywide responsibilities in the areas of housing and homelessness. Mayor Mel Lastman recognized that Jack had vast knowledge and extensive experience in this area, which he harnessed through a special task-force report called *Taking Responsibility for Homelessness* in January 1999. At the time, Toronto's homeless population was on the rise, with a temporary community called "Tent City" established on vacant waterfront industrial lands. Jack championed the cause and helped to find housing solutions that resulted in the placement of formerly homeless people into what was often their first apartment.

Perhaps what I most remember about Jack was his unwavering optimism. He always had a positive outlook and was confident that when people were brought together they could make a difference. He would have made an excellent mayor but he had a higher calling. When he left City Council for Ottawa, many sceptical councillors thought he was taking a huge risk. While most people wished him well they had no idea of the impact he would have on a national scale. He surprised a lot of people with his sheer passion, energy, and dedication to improving the lives of Canadians across the country. In my view, the results of the last federal election were in large part because of Jack.

His tragic passing touched all Canadians deeply because they felt they had lost a trusted friend. I recall how upset I was on hearing the news and I delivered a personal note to Olivia on their front porch that same morning. I also shared in the amazing experience of waiting in line for hours with so many others on Parliament Hill to pay my respects. I was very fortunate to meet with Olivia for a few moments as she came out to greet Canadians and was especially moved by the outpouring of public affection for Jack at Toronto's Nathan Phillips Square, as I joined the thousands of people walking down University Avenue for his final journey from City Hall.

He was a very special man who practised what he preached and whose memory will not fade in the hearts and minds of Canadians.

Working for the Possible
BRIAN O'KEEFE

While my memories of Jack date back to his early days on Toronto City Council in the 1980s, one distinctive memory is from the period after he was re-elected to Metro Council in 1994. He had been away from elected politics for a few years following his run for mayor of Toronto in 1991. At that time, I was the treasurer of CUPE Local 79 and was very active at Metro Hall at budget time, attempting to defend the interests of our members. In the spring of 1995, just before the election of Mike Harris's Conservative provincial government in June of that year, I was especially concerned about a serious attempt to erode social services. I worked very closely with the NDP caucus, including Jack and Olivia, throughout the budget session that year. My first inclination was to focus most of my energy on support from allies on Council with a view to preventing cuts of any kind. This was a laudable objective, but I quickly realized that that was not how things worked at Metro Council. This was a major learning moment for me.

In hindsight, I believe that we would have lost a lot more valuable social services that year without Jack's skilful leadership. Although I didn't fully appreciate it at the time, his outstanding ability to reach out and communicate with councillors of different persuasions was quite amazing. He determined with us in advance what he thought was possible to achieve and then he went to work to achieve it with total dedication.

He could sustain an argument with the likes of Mel Lastman just as readily as he could with his fellow NDP councillors. He also had an uncanny ability to persuade staff, such as then-Metro CAO Bob Richards, of the merits of his position. Once he knew where he was going on an issue, he was tireless in pursuit of his goal, even if it meant working long into the night. We didn't get everything we wanted that year, but we did achieve everything in the plan that we worked on with Jack.

The National Squash League
PAUL COPELAND

In 1977, at the urging of Steve Thomas, NDP fundraiser extraordinaire, six of us—most of whom had connections with the NDP—founded something modestly named the National Squash League. Initially we played on American-style courts and we always used American scoring. To equalize our games somewhat, each player was given a points handicap. On the model of the National Hockey League, four of our six players made it into the playoffs.

Years later the league expanded and, as an expression of our self-granted pomposity, it was renamed the Royal Canadian National Squash League. In choosing that name, we anticipated Prime Minister Harper's infatuation with the royals by about twenty-five years. Princess Margaret, unbeknownst to her, was our royal patron. Each year the Princess Margaret Trophy was given to the person who won a playoff game held between the two losers of the semifinals.

The exact moment we allowed a Toronto city councillor (perhaps at that time he was a Metro councillor) with roots in Quebec to join our league is lost in the mists of time. Jack was a formidable competitor. He played out of the Curzons SkyDome Club. From the league records that I still have, his handicap was -4, which ranked him among the better players in the league. His upper body development as a result of competitive swimming was impressive.

Jack was league champion in 1991–2 and 1992–3. However, the records are a trifle unclear on this point. As a result of the handicap scoring system, some of the better players ended up at the bottom of the league standings. The winner of the game between the two players with the worst records over the season was the Consolation Champion. The records show Jack was a Consolation Cup winner in 1992–3.

Campaigning: Early Signs
MICHAEL GOLDRICK

I was a candidate for City Council in the west end of Toronto in 1972 and was fortunate enough to recruit a large number of students and young activists for the "dog work" of canvassing, sign distribution, and telephoning. While they had huge energy and enthusiasm, they had little experience in campaign strategy and organization. But I do recall a somewhat brash young man fresh from community organizing for the Front d'action politique (FRAP) in Montreal appearing in the campaign office and offering quite urgently to take on some canvass organizing. I have to confess that initially I was slightly sceptical that his large, wide-brimmed leather hat and leather jacket would "fit" Ward 3 in heavily ethnic west Toronto. But before long—hours, not days—it was totally apparent that this was a guy who knew what he was about, knew how to assemble and keep together many first-time campaigners, and knew how to frame local issues and strategies in association with other strong personalities. This was a gift from election heaven that became a hallmark of Jack's future career.

Canvassing con brio
PETER TABUNS

I had canvassed for years; but until October 1990 I hadn't done apartment buildings and I hadn't canvassed with Jack.

He showed up on his bike, locked it to a fence in front of the building, and started us on the top floor. To my amazement he started knocking on doors four at a time, moving down the hall trying to rouse as many people as he could. In these buildings, many won't answer the doors at all, but Jack's ratio was right—he would get about one in four.

He was happiest when he could rouse four households at once and hold an impromptu public meeting right there in the hall. Then he would grandly introduce me as one of Toronto's leading environmentalists (definitely overselling the candidate), urge people to vote for me, leave me to answer questions, and move on to the next block of doors to try to rouse more residents to abandon their TV sets and join us in old-fashioned hallway electioneering.

When Jack ran to become mayor of Toronto in 1991, the election became highly polarized: Jack was either adored or pilloried. We shared office space during this campaign, as I was running for City Council. Throughout that demanding campaign, Jack's sense of humour seemed to fuel him day in and day out.

One morning he came into the office after campaigning at a subway stop in the east end. He was in great form and abuzz with a creative insult that had been dumped on him. He had been handing out flyers when a man came up to him to inquire if he was Jack Layton. (Maybe the button gave him away, I don't know.) Jack said that he was indeed himself. The voter then proclaimed that Jack was such a bad candidate that he "would not piss on your head if your brains were on fire." Jack was both amused and impressed with this novel insult and went through the office relating the story to roars of laughter.

Hallowe'en Monster
SARAH LAYTON

My husband loves Hallowe'en. We decorate the outside of our home and try to scare the neighbourhood kids. It's a strange tradition when I stop and think about it, but it sure is fun!

Growing up in downtown Toronto, my family always loved Hallowe'en, and my father took great joy in being a local attraction that night each year. He would bring out his special long, black Hallowe'en robe and put on a hairy monster mask that was certainly the most frightening thing any child in my old neighbourhood had ever seen. He would put on his very best creepy walk and terrifying voice to say "Come closer" to each young trick-or-treater, just as a bloodcurdling scream would come from the spooky sound-effects tape being played at full volume by the front door.

Little princesses, ghosts, and robots would tentatively walk up our pathway only to be frightened into running back to their parents, who waited, often laughing, on the sidewalk. Over the years, the young children would pride themselves on getting a little bit closer to our house than they had the previous year. This was a sign of being older and braver that was respected neighbourhood-wide.

Occasionally Dad would take off the mask to console a totally petrified preschooler, and my mother would always come out of the house to give each child a treat, whether or not they made it all the way to our monster man.

My brother and I often run into old friends from the neighbourhood, and they all remember how my dad got so into his role and how much fun they had daring each other to go up to him.

Over the last few years, my dad and Olivia would join my husband and me at our little haunted house—in full costume, of course. What a fun family and neighbourhood tradition. It's not so much about the haul of candy at the end of the night, but about the memorable childhood experience for anyone who dared to come by.

In Jack's Office
PETER EHRLICH

I remember just starting to work for Jack at City Hall. Although by 1999 I had already known him through my work at the White Ribbon Campaign, I did not know him well as a politician.

I often took care of his appointment calendar. Monday to Saturday was almost always blocked off for work from 7 AM to 11 PM. His work ethic was unbelievable. In all the years I worked for him, I saw him put his feet up to rest only once. When I walked into our office that day and saw him, head back, eyes closed, feet up, face to the sun, I stopped dead in my tracks, then slowly backed out of the office. That is how shocked I was.

Working in the same office as Jack at Toronto City Hall, I was privy to many of his meetings, often with his bitterest political opponents. After they left the office, I never once heard him say anything negative about those attending the meeting. Not once. And in all the years, I never heard him put anyone down. Of course, if it had to do with a social injustice, the injustice pissed him off. But he never made it personal. He would never call anyone a name. The man was truly about "peace, love, and understanding."

One time we were walking across City Hall plaza when a homeless man came up to us. He said, "Jack, I just wanted to thank you for all you've done for me." Now this guy had nothing to gain from saying something to Jack about his plight and the issue of homelessness. He was simply too poor, too homeless. That's when I really knew, without a scintilla of doubt, that Jack was the real deal.

Beating the Municipal Odds
FRANZ HARTMANN

"Let's not give up. We will still win this."

Those words ring with me a good eleven years after they were passionately spoken by Jack to a group of activists in July 2000. Some were from Kirkland Lake, a small town in northeastern Ontario. Others were from Toronto, including leaders from the city's environmental community. We were gathered in a committee room in Toronto City Hall, right after City Council had voted to give city staff the go-ahead to negotiate a contract with Rail Cycle North to ship Toronto's garbage to an abandoned, water-filled open-pit mine near Kirkland Lake. We were completely dejected because a powerful coalition of political interests (Toronto Mayor Mel Lastman, Ontario Premier Mike Harris), business interests (prominent Ontario investors with ties to Premier Harris and the world's largest waste-management company), and Toronto media were supporting the plan to ship Toronto's garbage to what became known as the Adams Mine.

Yet Jack urged us not to give up. He made it clear that the fight was not over and reminded us that the final negotiated contract still had to come back to City Council for approval. And, he said, we can still win this because it is a bad idea and because people in Ontario will speak up once they know what's at stake. His confidence was contagious—a typical reaction for a man whom I had known for almost a decade and worked with for more than two years as his environment advisor at City Hall.

People took Jack's confidence and embraced it like a warm blanket on a cold winter's night. For me, his words were comforting but part of me couldn't help doubting. I had been in politics long enough to know we were up against almost impossible odds, given the powerful people who obviously had locked up all the support they needed.

But my doubts—and, I suspect, the doubts others might have had—were no match for Jack's confidence and enthusiasm. In typical Jack style, he immediately began brainstorming what we could do between now and the fall City Council meeting. We talked about actions near the mine to get media and therefore public attention for the environmental dangers of shipping Toronto's garbage to Kirkland Lake. We talked about connecting with Torontonians and letting them know that shipping garbage to Kirkland Lake would make it much more difficult to increase waste diversion in Toronto, a practice an increasing number of Torontonians were embracing. By the end of the meeting, we all had our to-do lists and were once again full of resolve to keep fighting against this bad proposal.

Jack, of course, knew we were in a textbook David-and-Goliath fight. But he also knew that giving up guaranteed defeat. This constant optimism coupled with a seemingly endless capacity for work, especially with a dedicated team of people, was what made Jack one of the most effective public servants this country has ever seen. His entire life was dedicated to making his city, our country, and our planet a healthier and more socially equitable place. And he had fun, pretty well every day.

Jack's optimism didn't always win the day, as his death shows us. But it did help stop a bad proposal to ship Toronto's garbage to Adams Mine. Two and half months after that fateful meeting at City Hall we were all gathered again, this time to celebrate the defeat of the proposal. As it turned out, what brought down Goliath was a combination of on-the-ground activism and greed.

On the ground, a dedicated group of activists in Toronto and northern Ontario worked hard to get the Adams Mine story in front of the public. They were so successful that by the time the negotiated contract was in front of City Council in the fall of 2000, the national media and most Torontonians were paying close attention. Because of this intense public and media scrutiny, councillors who supported the plan were forced to remove a clause from the contract that would potentially have burdened Toronto residents with hundreds of millions of dollars in additional costs. Days after Council voted to remove the clause, Rail Cycle North—in particular

Waste Management Inc., the richest partner in the consortium—walked away from the deal. RCN made it clear the clause was necessary to guarantee its profits. Without the clause, the business case was gone. With the deal dead, Torontonians were spared a very expensive and environmentally damaging debacle. Instead, City Council embraced aggressive waste-diversion plans that have helped Toronto dramatically reduce the garbage it now sends to landfills.

I can say with absolute certainty none of this would have happened without Jack and his incredible work habits and tireless enthusiasm. Torontonians and Canadians owe him a large debt of gratitude for this and the many other victories he was key to. But Jack was never one to revel in praise or victory. With unfailing consistency, he began planning for the next opportunity to make the world a better place. And he would have told us, "Let's not give up. We will still win this."

Engaging the "Enemy"
BILL FREEMAN

Sometime in the early 1990s I was with a group of Toronto Island residents at Metro Hall listening to members of Metro Council debating some issue that concerned us. I can't for the life of me remember what was at stake, but I know we would never have had a chance to have it adopted without Jack Layton, then a Metro councillor, on our side. Predictably, the debate droned on, enlivened only by veiled insults about Island squatters. Jack made a valiant effort to defend our cause, but the motion failed.

After the meeting was adjourned, our group of Islanders gathered around Jack, complaining bitterly about the insults and how the issue was treated. Jack suddenly excused himself and went to talk to some right-wing councillors, the very ones who had just voted down our motion. I was appalled. How could Jack Layton, the very person who advocated our position and gave us leadership and encouragement, talk to this group of Neanderthals? I watched them chatting in an animated way. Jack was laughing. He seemed as happy with them as he was with us, his dedicated supporters. A few moments later Jack broke off his conversation and came back to our group. I couldn't stop myself. I just had to say something that showed my disapproval: "Jack, how could you talk to those guys after what they just did to us?"

"In this place you have to work with everyone if you want to get things done," he replied. "I'll need their votes the next time."

In that long-ago incident I learned something about Jack and the way he practised politics. His gentle reprimand was a reminder that to be effective you have to work with others, no matter where they stand on issues. You have to use all of your talents and charm if you want to make things happen. That was how Jack conducted his political and even his personal life, and it was one of the reasons he was so successful.

And Jack was a man of considerable talents and charm. On the election trail his smile lightened the room and he radiated a warmth towards everyone in it. It made us feel good just to be there participating in the event. Jack had an uncanny way of making people feel welcome, included, and important. His warmth and charm were as much a genuine part of him as his ability to understand and dissect such difficult issues as homelessness, affordable housing, and deep lake water cooling.

In municipal politics, Jack was effective because people liked him—even the right-wing councillors he worked with on Metro Council. That helped him gain their respect and attention. They listened to what he had to say, and because he knew the issues they grew to trust him and value his judgement. Everyone knew that Jack Layton was a leader of the left-wing group on Council, but there were many occasions when he could muster the votes to get issues he cared about adopted by Council.

Political parties dominate federal politics. Ottawa is an intensely partisan world where most politicians socialize only with members of their own party. Those in opposing parties are the enemy, scorned and ridiculed—targets of gibes and abuse in the House of Commons.

Jack refused to participate in that world. He repeated, "I will work with any party and anyone to further the interests of Canadians." In his view, he was elected to serve the people of Canada. He was the leader of the New Democratic Party and advocated its principles and policies, but he would work with anyone to help the people. That approach had an impact on Ottawa, and after his death it was often remarked that Jack raised the level of debate and helped others to leave behind the bitter wrangling that had characterized the House of Commons in recent years.

We know where Jack learned that approach. It was at Toronto City Hall and on Metro Council that he came to understand that politics involved working with people and trying to convince them of the virtues of a motion regardless of their political stripes. As he said, "You have to work with everyone if you want to get anything done."

The Day I Job Shadowed Jack Layton
RICHARD ZAJCHOWSKI

The next time you mouth that all-too-common disgust for politicians, I want you to think about Jack Layton.

It's Thursday, June 22, 2000. I'm staying at Jack and Olivia's in Toronto. Found my way to the shower before most everyone else. As Jack said, most of the house gets up later. But after showering and sans breakfast, Jack is heading out the door. Could I come with you and even shadow you? "Sure," says Jack, as he often does. His working day has started.

As we walk out into a beautiful morning, Jack makes a call on his cellphone to a fellow named Chris. Friendly chat about Jack not really being able to play golf but he would be there for the reception. Jack also wonders if Nancy, his sister, could sub for him. Then he gives Nancy a call and leaves a message on her answering machine. I chime in a hello from Zack. Zack and Jack are back together!

Jack then stops in at a locksmith to get ten keys cut—their house is an interim home to a long string of relatives, grad students, and other assorted folks, occasionally accompanied by their lovers.

By the way, the Chris he called is Chris Rudge, CEO of Quebecor. They just hired Brian Mulroney! As Jack says, great to be buddies with Brian M.'s boss! The golf discussion was around a White Ribbon golf tourney fundraiser with the Maple Leaf Old Timers and lots of the country's business elite. At some very exclusive golf club near London with green fees in the thousands. The Queen stays there when she visits Ontario.

I remind Jack that maybe a bit of breakfast would be

helpful, so we buy coffee and scones on the walk to work at City Hall.

Into City Hall and into Jack's office. Mark is answering phones. Franz and Richard are organizing various schedules and meetings as well as answering phones. Monica comes in and gets right to work on a project. Jack introduces me to everyone. Then off we head to a finance committee meeting, because Jack is concerned about getting homeless people a cool place during heat waves. Franz and Richard are circling Jack with messages and briefs. Into the meeting room, but the Hot Weather Advisory issue is way down the agenda, so back to the office. Jack makes phone calls while Richard and Franz come in and out with scheduling arrangements.

While reading his mail, Jack finds he's won an award from the Association of Energy Engineers! "More for the website," he says. I manage to do something useful when I notice on the closed-circuit TV that the Hot Weather Advisory is coming up next. So back to the meeting room, where a few members of the homeless committee make deputations regarding the need to care for the homeless and other forgotten citizens who suffer and can even die when the weather turns viciously steamy. Jack anchors their deputations with a motion to refer this issue to the next level. Chicago and Philadelphia created similar programs after a number of their citizens died in heat waves. Surprisingly to me, there is some scepticism even about the need for any measures. I can understand why some councillors express concern about camping in parks intended for everyone's recreation, but trying to discredit the whole Hot Weather Advisory endeavour seems frighteningly cynical and callous. The motion passes five to three. Scary that three councillors could vote against such a motion.

Outside in the hall, Jack debriefs and strategizes with the homeless committee folk. Then TV and radio interviews regarding the homeless. After that a quiet young reporter asks Jack about hydro rates policy. Sounds like Jack and the other Toronto Hydro folks have outflanked the Harris government on plans to privatize Toronto Hydro into the hands of their cronies. Jack wants a copy because he can put that too on the website. Then back to Jack's office for an interview about the spiritual and economic aspects of homelessness and greed. More phone calls and briefings, as well as schedule changes due to the Gillian Hadley murder-suicide press conference. Jack is there to represent the White Ribbon Campaign. Somewhere, he had to find time to think about what he'd say. More phone calls.

Up to Council area for a Citytv interview about the murder-suicide case. While he's there, a woman who met Jack on a plane comes by about some issue—supporting a cancer camp perhaps. While walking back to the office for a meeting, he passes by a reception for bicycle transportation. I think Jack manages in those few moments to both appreciate at least two other people's work and make plans for future initiatives.

I suggest to Franz that I should try to get some food for Jack—by now it's 12:20 and he hasn't stopped or eaten anything but a scone! However, Franz points out that there is food at the reception—danishes and pineapples wouldn't be to Jack's taste nor, I might add, would they be nutritionally useful.

Down to a meeting with a lawyer (I think) named Jeff, in a nice suit. Jack has on his trademark swagger and an open shirt and jeans. So many "suits" present, but Jack doesn't care, not intimidated at all. The suits all know Jack has immense power—great to see them kowtowing. Interview with Jeff over, the three of us, including Jeff, walk over to a dreary press conference about the terrible murder-suicide. Jack and a fellow named Gary make excellent and moving presentations. Talk to Franz and we marvel at Jack's ability to motivate folks. So what am I doing to help women? At least I could call my MP about changes to criminal procedures. Everyone has the right to safety and security. This was a disaster waiting to happen. The estranged husband had already attacked a few times before. Restraining orders don't work. Jack discusses ways to get useful White Ribbon info onto the Web.

Out of the conference room and Jack says hi to a cleaning lady who likes to sing soprano arias that Jack appreciates. On the street, people say hello to Jack—"keep up the good work"—including Buzz Hargrove, who happens to be passing by.

It's now 2 PM and Jack finally realizes he's hungry. So over to the Sheraton for a steak and a lunchtime (for Jack and Franz and me) interview with a columnist, who is happy to see Jack and just as keen as Jack on environmental issues. Columnist enthuses about the chance Toronto has, with garbage disposal hearings imminent (i.e., in one hour), to use methane recovery and energy cogeneration to achieve a triple win: less garbage to be shipped (if organics are separated out), methane producing energy, and job creation. Also CO^2/ greenhouse gas reduction due to less transport of garbage.

Jack talks to columnist about retrofitting Toronto and the economics of same. He was instrumental in getting two large funds set up so that other municipalities can learn from Toronto, where retrofitting is paid for out of future energy savings. They already retrofit 4 per cent plus of the commercial buildings in Toronto. Paul Martin is getting keen on Jack's idea of retrofitting the whole country!

Back to City Hall, where Jack is working on getting these more environmental ways of dealing with garbage on the table at the very big (full Council) hearing on garbage disposal. On the way up, Mayor Mel Lastman and his coterie step into the tiny elevator with Jack and me. Jack, of course, introduces me all around.

At the hearings Jack asks questions, works on his mail, gets letters done, and occasionally does interviews on the stairs. So many suits, so much power, so much money I could feel it.

I finally have to leave at 5 PM.

All this today within the context of a nasty harassment campaign of untruths and threats to Olivia, his wife, regarding the homeless riots in T.O. and her role on the police board.

It is 10:30 PM and Jack's still not back. Isn't he just the picture of a lazy, sleazy, cynical politician?

Jack happily lives in a funky, three-storey rowhouse that has a panoply of boarders and relations and at least two cats. He makes about $60,000 a year, and doesn't even own a car!

Note: Jack asked me at the time to type this up so he could put it on the Web. I procrastinated. Now I can't.

Focus on the Issues
JOE MIHEVC

Jack, Olivia, and I sat on the new City Council from 1997 to 2002, when Jack became NDP leader. At Council I sat with Olivia immediately on my right side and Jack a few seats over on my left. Between Jack and me sat three councillors, one of whom was Rob Ford, now Toronto's mayor. Immediately in front of us was prominent North York NDP councillor Howard Moscoe.

A few characteristics about Jack struck me and stay with me to this day. First, Jack never "made it personal" with Rob Ford. Clearly, they had absolutely nothing in common politically. Nonetheless, Jack would find common ground with Ford discussing sports or talking about federal Conservatives they both knew. Jack would sometimes make a joke, but he never denigrated a person. His was an argument about an issue and it remained at that level. The fights would be intense—for example whether to send Toronto's garbage to Adams Mine. Jack knew who the enemy was and what their arguments were. But he never fought them on personal grounds. Jack's approach helped build various coalitions at City Hall and beyond, because it ensured that the door was always open on another issue.

A second very clear memory of Jack was how damn hard he worked. He always had his computer at his desk in the Council chamber, and if he wasn't speaking or meeting with someone in the members' lounge, he was typing on his computer. When Council was over, even if it went well into the evening, he would often go back to his office to do more work. The work of social justice drove him passionately and endlessly. I have been to Jack and Olivia's home many times, and we've shared many drinks and meals, always in the context of the work that we were gathering. Socializing for its own sake was not something they did; it was woven into the projects they were working on. Socializing fit into the work, and made it fun and engaging.

Political and social change was a vocation for Jack. He believed that human beings could build a better world and he spent each and every moment—whether it was social, sports, arts and culture, and even his own funeral when you think about it—infusing us with a sense of political purpose.

If there is any pattern to understanding the basic issues and political predisposition that Jack carried in his years as a city councillor, it was being the voice of the underdog. Whether it was smoking or gay and lesbian issues in the 1980s, public health work on AIDS or men against violence against women in the 1990s, Jack had a way of diving head-first into the public discourse. Sometimes, especially in his younger years, he was brash and even abrasive in pushing an issue. Later, especially as leader of the NDP, his speaking style matured as he became more visionary and inclusive.

His work on homelessness and poverty demonstrated his struggle for the underdog. In the 1990s, Toronto, like much of the rest of Canada, really did not know what to do with people who were homeless. Poverty was on the rise in Toronto, and the crisis was resulting in more people sleeping on the streets. The public debate was whether to use police to sweep them off the street or to build shelters, provide support, and ultimately build more social housing. In Toronto, crowds gathered each night around City Hall to sleep. Some members of Council promoted a punitive approach to dealing with people on the street and those sleeping at City Hall. Jack would have none of it.

One memory that captures Jack's compassion was his friendship with a homeless person who hung around City Hall in those days. Jack embraced him every time they met. The formality of the occasion did not matter. Jack would introduce him as his friend, and with his classic grin invite him into his circle. I met this fellow at Jack's funeral. He was looking much better and explained to me that it was Jack who inspired him to get his life together.

Jack as a protagonist for the underdog was evident in another encounter I had with a man in Nathan Phillips Square during the days when the chalk tributes were being inscribed. This gentleman was from South Africa, and had been imprisoned with Nelson Mandela during the apartheid years. He eventually came to Toronto and worked here for Nelson Mandela and the African National Congress (ANC), which Jack supported when the ANC had its office on Danforth Avenue. He cried as he spoke of how he loved Jack and how nothing would keep him away from the square and from honouring the solidarity that Jack showed in the anti-apartheid struggle.

Bananas Say It All
DEREK LEEBOSH

From the moment I first moved to Toronto in 1981 to go to university, my path and Jack Layton's kept intersecting. I canvassed a poll for him when he was first elected to City Council in 1982 and gradually we accumulated a number of mutual friends. Over the years, as I began a career as a public-opinion researcher, Jack and I had numerous inter-actions, two of which will always stand out for me.

Sometime in the late 1990s, I was at a fundraiser for some good but alas forgotten cause. As is often the case at such events, there was a silent auction where one could bid on various items—one of which was a two-hour guided tour of the Toronto Port Lands on a tandem bicycle with Jack Layton, followed by a dim sum lunch in Chinatown. I put in a bid of $35, fully expecting to have a bidding war and to be outbid in the end. I was both pleased and slightly embarrassed that no one outbid me. In those days Jack was a Metro councillor who had run for mayor of Toronto once and for Parliament twice. He had lost each time, so I suppose that a few hours of "face time" with him wasn't sought after the way it was destined to be in later years.

Despite my bargain-basement bid, Jack was a good sport and his office called me to set up the tour. I met him at his house on a beautiful sunny Sunday morning in the autumn. I had never been on a tandem bicycle before and was surprised to learn how fast they go with two people pedalling. I still have a vivid memory of that bike trip along the waterfront and through the Port Lands. At every red light Jack would turn and give me his enthusiastic commentary from the front seat, pointing out where new film studios and other developments were planned. He was truly in his element, riding a tandem bicycle and showing off one of his favourite parts of his city. In retrospect it was an iconic moment. Afterwards, we had dim sum with Olivia and his then-teenage kids and found out that we were both "foodies" in addition to having been Anglo-Montrealers. We also discovered that, coincidentally, some years earlier he had lived in the very house I was then renting.

Fast forward about eight or nine years. By now Jack had become leader of the NDP during the minority Paul Martin government and we ran into each other on a Friday afternoon at Pearson Airport. We both needed a taxi into the city and there was a huge lineup, so we decided to share a cab. Several people recognized him and wanted to cede their place in line to him, but he would have none of it; so we waited our turn and talked about the latest political developments. For the first half of the ride he asked me about my impressions of how the NDP was doing and what it would take to gain momentum and to what extent I thought then-Opposition Leader Stephen Harper would be a formidable opponent.

Suddenly the conversation somehow segued into talking about shopping for groceries in Kensington Market, which was close to where he lived. Jack talked about a fruit and vegetable shop in the market that sold twelve varieties of bananas. For a few minutes in his life as a high-profile national politician, the most exciting thing in the world for him was the fact that, in this society where so much biodiversity is being lost, one shop was selling *twelve* types of bananas, each one a different size, colour, and flavour and each to be used for different dishes. For that fleeting moment, what had happened that day in Question Period or in caucus didn't matter—one shop was doing its part to maintain biodiversity and reminding us that there were at least twelve different kinds of bananas.

When I think back to those two personal anecdotes as well as other occasions over the years when I met up with Jack, I recall the impression he made on me, less as a public figure than as a great personality. In his everyday life he was always able to take the ordinary and make it extraordinary.

3

Walking the Walk

Beginning with his work on Toronto Council, Jack found himself engaged in all sorts of grassroots projects—food banks, organizations to combat homelessness or deal with diversity and gender issues. He brought practical proposals to the Council's attention, but also worked outside the formal political structure, lending a hand wherever it was needed, picking up a guitar at a fundraising event or an auctioneer's gavel to support local—and eventually nationwide—causes. He strategized with groups as diverse as the local FoodShare to those supporting migrant workers. For Jack, paying lip service to an issue was never going to be enough. He needed to be involved in a practical way that would change things.

The Politics of Potential
KEVIN CHIEF

In 2010, I ran as the NDP candidate in a federal byelection in Winnipeg North. The popular longtime NDP member of Parliament, Judy Wasylycia-Leis, had stepped down to run for mayor of Winnipeg. I was a young, first-time candidate going up against a popular eighteen-year incumbent MLA. Jack came to Winnipeg several times to campaign with me in the leadup to and during that election. It was under those unique circumstances that I got to know our federal leader.

From the beginning I was struck by how genuine he was and how effortlessly he connected with people from all backgrounds. You could tell that he really enjoyed people and that warmth came across to them. He put people at ease and made them feel that their story mattered. He taught us that we had to work hard but that politics had to be fun too. I was grateful for all the time Jack spent campaigning with me and the lessons he taught me about communicating with people on the doorstep and handling media.

The boundless energy and commitment he showed during that time was a lesson in itself for a new candidate trying to enter public life. He was a relentless campaigner; as soon as we finished one event he was cheerfully ready to go on to the next—all this when Jack was undergoing treatment for prostate cancer. Whenever I was out door-knocking and became tired and didn't want to keep going, all I had to do was think about Jack and how he kept going in the face of much greater problems.

Jack understood that politics could be about potential— the potential we see in individuals, the potential we see in one another, and the potential we see in communities. He understood that politics wasn't just about getting votes for today but about building relationships that stood up over time. You saw that reflected at his funeral, in the diversity of the relationships he had throughout the country. He had a tremendous impact on people. There was room for everybody in Jack's Canada—nobody would be left behind. Everyone could make a contribution in their own way to making our country a better place to live.

When I lost that 2010 byelection I was very disappointed, of course, but Jack helped me through that difficult time. He said, "Kevin, maybe you didn't win the byelection, but don't forget about all the wins you had—the people you met, the connections you made, and all the things you learned." It was Jack who reminded me of all those important wins, of all the people we had become friends with, how we were able to engage first-time voters, and how we united a community for causes we all believed in. These were all very real wins that Jack never let me lose sight of.

I like to think of this story of Jack's "wins" as teachings that laid a strong foundation for our team. It was those very same wins that allowed us to enjoy success in the Manitoba provincial election in 2011, when I became the MLA for Point Douglas. The lessons we had learned and the sense of belonging and relationships we had developed in the byelection allowed us to generate 350 volunteers for our campaign and inspire 1,100 new voters to come out and be a part of the democratic process. Thanks, Jack!

One Issue at a Time
DI McINTYRE

I remember walking with Jack as part of the ARMX Arms Show protest walk in 1988. I was pleased that he was here in my neighbourhood, joining in this protest against the proliferation of arms and the use of City of Ottawa property to promote weapons. The protest did help to inspire a bylaw banning such shows. During the walk, my daughter Leia rode on my shoulders, then on Jack's, as we proceeded down Bank Street towards Lansdowne Park.

Jack had been living in Toronto since the early 1970s and was taking an active part in his community. I'd been in Ottawa since 1968, an activist for community well-being and a member of Canadian Voice of Women for Peace. As we walked, we shared ideas about the state of the world, poverty, homelessness, discrimination, corporate greed, the misguided notion that the use of weapons could solve problems, the impact of wars on the environment, the misguided use of resources, etc. Jack turned to me and asked why I was not a member of the NDP, then added, "You'll join some day. The best NDPers come to the party one issue at a time."

A Visit
SHAWN A-IN-CHUT ATLEO

When I remember Jack, there are many moments, exchanges, and talks that come to mind. But the one that I recall most vividly was a simple, yet poignant visit.

My home is Ahousaht, a small village off the coast of Vancouver Island that is part of Clayoquot Sound. We are

Nuu-chah-nulth and continue to be guided by our trad-itional governing, cultural, and spiritual practices. Yet, not unlike every First Nation from coast to coast to coast, we have been affected and even traumatized by dispossession, displacement, and policies that caused serious and lasting harm.

In 2005, our village was overwhelmed by suicide attempts and two deaths. As we struggled to deal with this situation, the community and hereditary leadership came together and recognized that we needed to call for help. We reached out to all of our neighbours, to British Columbians, and to all of Canada. Many remarkable people answered this call. Jack and Olivia were among the first.

Shortly after a simple email message, Jack and Olivia arrived at Tofino on a foggy morning in late August. They hopped aboard the *Ahousaht Pride* community seabus to come to our village. With no particular set program, my wife Nancy and I met them as they arrived. As we wandered up from the dock, we saw that my Gran Flossy (Florence Atleo), who lived nearby, was hard at work canning salmon. Jack was immedi-ately curious and drawn in to watch and to learn.

Gran invited him in the back door of her small home into her kitchen. Without pausing, she carried on with her work, explaining everything she was doing as Jack listened eagerly. She meticulously prepared the salmon, carefully placing the bones and skin—what others would throw away—in a pot. As she explained, this would later be transformed into a rich and satisfying soup for the entire family.

Gran had also broiled some salmon roe with salt and pepper to eat while she worked. She motioned to it, offering it to us with a shy smile. In our village this is a special treat called "niiktin," but for the uninitiated it has a very strong taste. Jack, though, was honoured by the offer and eagerly came forward to try it. He savoured it slowly and smiled his appreciation to Gran.

We carried on through the village towards the band office. Jack was at ease, meeting and visiting with people along the road. We arrived at a meeting with the council and joined them for fresh salmon sandwiches and fishhead soup for lunch. Jack and Olivia listened to presentations and exchanged information and questions about Ahousaht. Throughout, Jack listened attentively to the challenges in the community and also to our hopes for opportunity, recovery, and growth. Jack understood that he was not there to bring solutions but rather to help build support for the solutions that our community was searching for from within.

Jack and Olivia later spent time at my home sharing stories and perspectives. I gave Jack a headband made of cedar and explained that it was made from, in our language, "utlyuu," the same word from which my family name Atleo is derived. He appreciated the gift and wanted to learn more and so I explained that the bark is harvested very carefully and only at a certain time of the year to ensure that the tree is not damaged in any way and continues to grow strong and support life. In later years, while we didn't discuss it, I always noticed that Jack kept that headband in a prominent place in his office.

Jack's great gift, so well demonstrated that summer day, was his genuine openness to joining people in their own experience. Through the connection established with my village and with many other First Nations across Canada, Jack was able to advance support for our issues grounded in this critical understanding.

After a full day, as they prepared to depart, Jack shook my hand and looked at me squarely. "Shawn," he said, "thank you. Please call me and I'll always do whatever I can." A simple phrase but one that proved true, time and again, as Jack never failed to take a phone call and he never failed to listen. Jack became a friend to many First Nation leaders because he grew to understand the challenges on a personal level. So too, Jack became a great leader for the country because he took the time to visit and the time to listen.

Getting There
DI McINTYRE

Although Jack was a good driver, he only owned one car—a high-school graduation present from his parents, making good on their promise to buy him one if he got an average of over 90 per cent on his final exams. That used Sunbeam spent most of its first summer in the garage in Hudson in need of repairs, for which his mother says they were thankful. On principle, Jack never owned another car. He used his bike to travel locally and had a bicycle built for two for his honeymoon and for touring with Olivia.

As leader of the NDP, Jack was allocated a government car and a parking spot on the west side of Parliament's Centre Block. Jack did not want a car, but it could not be given back; so, like the Sunbeam, it mostly sat idle, except when Jack and his staff needed to attend functions and meetings together.

Jack invited me to go to Rideau Hall for his induction into the Privy Council. He asked if I would drive and suggested that I meet him and Ed Broadbent at the back entrance of the Justice Building. I picked them up and we headed for the Governor General's residence. As I headed towards the back gate to park, Jack and Ed redirected me to go through the main entry and up the front driveway. As I pulled up to the front entrance, Jack chuckled. My old green VW Golf, he said, was symbolically perfect as the "official NDP limo."

Jack had a great rapport with taxi drivers. Deb Duffy told me that he had his favourite drivers in various cities on his speed-dial. They always greeted Jack warmly as a friend; he listened to their stories, asked about their families, and tipped generously. A neighbour recalls that Jack sometimes offered her a lift in his cab and listened intently to the public-health issues that she raised en route.

In Ottawa, Jack usually biked down Bank Street from the Glebe to Parliament Hill. People waved; he waved back. He sometimes talked about what he had noticed along the way. When Olivia's bike was added to the morning commute, people often recognized her funky bike with the milk-crate carrier decorated with flowers.

On August 24, 2011, two days after Jack died, I had been asked to come to the CBC for a 7 AM interview. I cycled downtown and, as I rode, I thought about what Jack saw every day as the city woke up. People starting their days, homeless people moving from their sleeping spots in doorways and alleys, signs, graffiti, potholes in unmarked cycling lanes. I thought about how Jack would take it all in and how it would inform his ideas about what real progress meant.

Sometimes Jack and Olivia would walk to Parliament Hill in the morning, especially if they were flying out that day. My mom recounts a story told to her by a young woman. She had been standing at a bus stop, and was surprised to see Jack and Olivia walking down Bank Street. They smiled. She dashed after them and cut them off, grinning. Jack stopped, smiled back, and said, "Hi. Is there something I can do for you?" She just replied excitedly, "I talked to Jack Layton!"

When I recounted this story to Olivia she said, yes, that happened all the time—everybody wanted to talk to Jack and he was always receptive and welcoming.

Fore!
JOE MIHEVC

In 2002, while still a councillor, Jack was part of a group including David Miller, Myer Siemiatycki, and myself, that had taken to playing golf a few Sunday mornings at the Don Valley municipal course. We were, more often than not, the first ones off the tee. Jack could even make playing golf a political enterprise. A few days before a game, he came to me—I was chair of the Board of Health at the time—with an idea to do a press conference about restricting pesticides. He'd do it on the putting green. "It would make a great backdrop for TV," he enthused, "and by doing it on a Sunday, we can set the pace for the week's media cycle."

A Chance Meeting
MICHAEL P. O'HARA

In 2009 I had the good fortune to be invited by my sister Mary Margaret to sing a duet of the classic ballad "Barbara Allen" with her for the annual Riverdale Share Concert in Toronto's east end. It was a lot of fun. What added to the glow of that day was a chance meeting with Jack Layton at an after-dinner party at the home of Susan Baker, producer of the Riverdale Share Concert. Quite the celebrity Toronto politician and then-leader of the NDP, yet I thought, "What a cool, down-to-earth guy."

As we talked, I asked if he had heard of the candlelight vigil for global warming that was taking place at Queen's Park that evening. He answered, "Of course, and I plan to attend. My son Michael is photographing it and is one of the organizers." I told him I was planning on attending as well, whereupon he asked, "Can I catch a ride with you?" He was never one to burn his own carbon, so I was obliged to let him tag along, taking full responsibility for the CO^2 emissions and freeing him of carbon guilt.

On the drive there I mentioned that as a union driver in the film industry I had driven a lot of celebrities over the years, but never the leader of a Canadian political party. I added that I loved that he didn't mind pulling up to a political demonstration at Queen's Park in a small econo-sized vehicle. He laughed as he rolled down the window and told the RCMP to let my car enter the grounds, parting the barricades.

Once inside, Jack watched with the other candlelight demonstrators as the organizers talked about how far the movement against global warming had grown in recent months and what was being done from across the globe. Michael Layton then asked his father to speak and introduced Jack as one of Canada's founding activists against global warming. Yet what struck me about his speech was his humility. He said that so many others had come before him and still work today for the same causes, and that, yes, these demonstrations and the recent candlelight vigils across the globe have made a great difference.

I guess the only thing I would have changed about that night is this: it would have been nice to have walked to the candlelight vigil with Jack, and to have a little more time with the great humanitarian and generous human spirit that he was.

The Auctioneer
DI McINTYRE

Jack's talents as an auctioneer for charity are well known. (He'd met Olivia at a charity auction in Toronto.) But he was also willing to support good causes beyond his home turf. Long before Jack had a national profile, he accepted my invitation and made a special trip from Toronto to Ottawa to be our auctioneer at a local fundraiser: the Mutchmor School Council had organized the auction to raise money for library books.

Jack's enthusiasm was infectious, and it had an effect on bidders. His professional patter urged the bidding upward, often well beyond the estimates. That day, he auctioned a $200 gift certificate for McKeen's Metro grocery store for $250. (The donor, Jim McKeen, good-naturedly agreed to a proviso by buyer Frank Augustyn that he'd be able to use it to purchase a certain type of caviar.) The fundraiser exceeded its objectives and the school council spread the goodwill by donating a portion of the proceeds to Viscount Alexander Public School for its library.

Jack and I celebrated with a group of other parents over a beer.

The Company We Keep
BILL BLAIKIE

One morning in 1985 or so I was standing on Laurier Avenue in Ottawa waiting for a bus on my way to Parliament Hill. I can't remember for sure, but I may even have had my thumb out—I did sometimes hitchhike to the Hill. It always made for interesting dialogue as I tried to avoid revealing that I was a member of Parliament. In any event, this one morning a big black car pulled up beside me, the window came down, and a voice said, "Jump in, Bill!" I bent down and looked in the car. It was Bob Layton, Jack's father, who at that time was a cabinet minister in the recently elected government of Brian Mulroney.

I did jump in, and recall a very pleasant conversation with a very pleasant man, who asked me if I knew his son, Jack, who was involved with the NDP in Toronto and was a city councillor there. I replied that I knew of Jack, but hadn't met him. There was a gentle pride in his voice when he spoke about Jack, and also an appreciation of the humour or irony of the difference in their politics. I believe he used the same expression that years later I would hear Jack use about him, that they had each fallen into bad company, but were good people nonetheless.

I did not actually meet Jack Layton until 2002 when as president of the Federation of Canadian Municipalities he made a presentation to the NDP caucus about the import-ance of more attention to the needs of Canadian cities. I told him the story of my ride to the Hill with his dad, and it became a sort of touchstone story between us, as his father passed away in May of that year. What I did not know then was that Jack would soon be my successful rival for the leadership of the federal NDP, and that he would be carry-ing his father's parliamentary pin in his pocket when he won.

After the leadership race, and after I had become the parliamentary leader of the NDP until such time as Jack was able to enter the House, the idea emerged that we gather in my office for a drink some night to get to know each other better. We did, and a bottle of single malt later, I believe we did know each other better in a positive way. As the night wore on, I came to know more than I may have wanted to know about how Jack had triumphed in the leadership, as he unabashedly laid bare his strategies and his way with the media, but also the admiration that he had for his father.

For my part I warned him about the downside of various positions and approaches that he cherished. I made the claim, for example, that not all microphones and cameras were equal, and that some might be better to pass up. To his credit, as his years as leader progressed, he was not unwilling to tell me on occasion that I had been right about a few things. The critical thing was that he ultimately persuaded me of the possibility that the next parliament would be a minority Liberal one, that my experience would be important to him, and that I should abandon any thoughts I might have of calling it a day after twenty-five years.

Jack was particularly animated that night when telling the story of the United Church youth group his father had led in Hudson, Quebec. Jack had belonged to the group, and they called themselves, at the elder Layton's suggestion, the "Infusers," whose mission it was to infuse everything with the spirit of social justice and other Christian virtues. Jack missed his father, and as he came to know that the end might be near in the summer of 2011, I am sure that the idea of possibly encountering his father again on the other side of the mystery of death was something that brought him some comfort.

Jack and I were always going to sample another bottle of single malt together, but we never got around to it. Perhaps we didn't need to. We had already established, only a year apart as we were, that we were both products of the same church, the same sixties counterculture, and the same hope for the NDP that it could become more than it had been. I was glad that I was able to strike up a good relationship in the aftermath of the leadership race, and do what I could to help him make our common hope come true. Our last face-to-face discussion, at the federal convention in June 2011, was about what I might do to be of assistance to him as the new leader of the Official Opposition. I wish we could have had the follow-up conversation.

Linking the Generations
DI McINTYRE

As children we were embraced by family, who lived in relatively close proximity in Hudson, Montreal, and Cowansville. Over the years, most of us moved away for jobs or to attend various schools, but the Layton cousins and our children have continued to get together.

When my daughter Leia was two, we had a family reunion here in Ottawa. A photo shows our offspring lined up by height—Jack's Michael and Sarah are the tallest. We have had numerous gatherings since then, in Milton, Toronto, Ottawa, Cornwall, and Kingston, Ontario. Four generations gathered in Burlington to celebrate the sixtieth wedding anniversary of Great-Uncle Jack and Auntie Jean England. Naturally, Jack and his sister Nancy played guitar and led a singsong, and we snapped lots of family photos. Jack and Olivia brought cartons of songbooks. Jack also brought copies of *Rise Up Singing* to my mom's eightieth birthday party and again played guitar so that we could all sing along. He kept a couple of cartons of these songbooks in his office—always ready for a singsong.

Most of the family gathered in Montreal in April 2008 for the 100th anniversary of the founding of the Montreal Association for the Blind and for Canada Post's official launch of the first-ever braille stamp and commemorative envelope honouring our great-grandfather, Philip E. Layton. The Honourable Jack was the centrepiece of the day and was presented with a lovely framed commemorative piece. He turned and handed it to my mom, the oldest surviving Layton, and said, "Here Auntie Joan, you should have this, not me," and asked that a photo be taken of all of us.

Jack had also been also asked to speak at Concordia University at a celebration of the 100th anniversary of the Montreal Association. I had been identifying people in old archival photos for the celebration display and had written Jack's speech. I was touched when he asked me to replace him as the speaker: "Cuz, you are the one who should be doing this. You know the history and, as the oldest cousin, you should be the one to tell our family story."

Once, Jack and my mom (Joan) were visiting Jack's mom in Florida. Jack knew all the great eating spots, and he and Joan headed out to a beachside oyster bar where they devoured more oysters than I want to consider in my lifetime. Jack was impressed that Auntie Joan could keep up with him.

Jack invited my mom to several Remembrance Day events at the National War Memorial in Ottawa. One cold November 11 she remembers Jack's providing her with a cozy lap blanket. On another Remembrance Day, I drove Mom to meet Jack at the flame and he escorted her, pushing her wheelchair down Sparks Street, proudly telling reporters that his Auntie Joan had served overseas as a dancer with the Canadian Legion All-Stars Concert Party, which had entertained our Second World War troops in eastern Canada,

Germany, Belgium, France, and England.

Jack had helped his brothers and sister arrange a great family gathering for his mom's eightieth birthday on June 25, 2011. The party brought together all of the Layton and Steeves clan and Auntie Do was surrounded by adorable children, many in cute smocked outfits she had made. Sadly, that night Jack couldn't attend: he was standing on guard for all of us, filibustering overnight in Parliament on behalf of locked-out postal workers. Jack's mom was disappointed but understood that he had to be with his newly-formed Official Opposition caucus during this important protest. We all gathered around a speakerphone when he called to share birthday wishes and joined in singing "Happy Birthday."

Glaciers, Grizzlies, and Jack
NEIL HARTLING

River guides from around the world know of the Alsek as North America's wildest river. Flowing through the world's largest nonpolar glaciated region and within sight of some of Canada's tallest mountains, it is the closest landscape in Canada to the Himalayas.

Jack came with Olivia on northern expeditions to unwind, reflect on issues, and recharge his batteries. Unlike many VIPs they did not come with their own exclusive entourage. On the Alsek, it was Jack and Olivia with a filmmaker friend, Nancy Tong, and they signed on to join a group of strangers. You can imagine the surprise of the other group members when this highly recognizable pair showed up at the beginning of the trip. There had been no selective "screening" and the personalities and political leanings of the group were wide and varied, yet Jack and Olivia quickly fit in comfortably as fellow travellers. While "star-struck" by the pair, the group respected their desire for some personal time and a bond of camaraderie formed.

On a two-week expedition, you are in a close community. Camping, sharing meals, rafting, hiking, and socializing around the campfire, you get the measure of a person.

In spite of his tremendous public stature, he fit in like a regular member of the group, putting people at ease and connecting with them as individuals. The man was truly brilliant, but able to engage with people at all levels.

Around the campfire it was clear that he was a born leader. Of course he had stories to tell, often self-deprecating. He brought his travel guitar with a memory full of popular old standards and would also play riffs, while encouraging others to come up with freestyle verse. It was a lot of fun and, most important, it showed how natural it was for him to help others shine.

Perhaps the most telling demonstration of his integrity occurred one day in the raft when someone mentioned one of the scandalous scenarios about an opposing party member recently in the news. It could have been an easy segue to a story rich in gossip and innuendo, but Jack didn't take the bait. He was quick to downplay it, saying it was unfortunate, and he moved the talk to a positive topic.

Grizzlies were abundant, although never a threat. We saw twenty-nine on that trip, most spotted by Urs, a Swiss fellow whose name uncannily translates as "bear"! Jack loved studying them from a distance.

As it flows to the Gulf of Alaska, the Alsek River tumbles through glacier-carved mountain valleys, beneath stunning spires and sprawling glaciers. The Tweedsmuir Glacier had recently surged, likely as a result of increased flow of meltwater underneath, nearly blocking the powerful river. Here we used a helicopter for the eleven-kilometre portage around the glacier and Turnback Canyon. While waiting for the heli, Nancy filmed Jack speaking about the rapidly melting glaciers as evidence of climate change. The resulting footage became the popular YouTube video *Melting Glaciers—Climate Change and the Alsek River*. It shows how attuned he was to the issues facing us, not only as a country but as a planet. I still enjoy rewatching that video and bringing back fond memories of that trip with Jack.

Matchmaking
MARILYN CHURLEY

I want to tell you about Jack as a friend. We were close political allies, as we represented the same area for many years in different capacities, but the stories I want to tell are reflections of a magnificent and joyous friendship.

I first met Jack in the early 1980s when I was a single mom living in South Riverdale in Toronto and involved in local housing and environmental issues. Jack didn't even represent this area back then, but he was always there to support me on these issues. In 1988, when I was first elected to Toronto City Council for Ward 8, Jack was a veteran of City Council, having been elected in 1982. He took me under his wing and I considered myself lucky to have such a great mentor. But Jack being Jack, we ended up mentoring each other. As he showed me the ropes at City Hall, he picked my brain for more information on the environmental movement, what support single moms like me needed, and how men could help address violence against women.

We also quickly discovered that we had a lot in common. We were both cyclists, we were passionate about the same issues—and we liked a good glass of red wine from time to time! It was the beginning of a very good friendship that deepened over the years.

Jack's connection to his friends was important to him and he stayed in touch no matter how busy he was. He had entered the date of my birthday in his BlackBerry and, without fail, if we were unable to get together, at some point on my birthday a call would come from Jack: there he'd be, doing a Marilyn Monroe rendition of "Happy Birthday." I know this happened for other friends as well.

I have many fond memories of Jack and me sitting in local restaurants after wrapping up meetings and events in the riding. Of course being with Jack in public was always a bit of a challenge because people kept approaching him to shake his hand and to have their pictures taken with him. People loved being in his orbit because he was so welcoming and made everyone feel that who they were and what they did was important and valued. But we always managed to carve out some time alone where we would share what was happening in our lives. At some point during most of those late-night meetings, Jack would pull out his cellphone and I'd hear him say, "Hi Luv, where are you? I'm in a restaurant with Marilyn Churley—do you want to join us?" No matter where Jack was and whom he was with, Olivia was never far from his thoughts.

Jack loved to play Cupid for his single friends. He explained that he was so happy in his relationship with Olivia that he couldn't stand to see his friends without a partner. He meant partner in the full sense of the word, like the kind of relationship he had with Olivia—a romantic partnership for sure, but also one of shared values, love of politics, and fighting for causes like peace and justice.

One icy night in early February 1998, Jack and I were having a drink at the Black Swan in our riding. My marriage of seventeen years had ended and I was complaining about how much I hated the dating scene. I told Jack about a recent unfortunate encounter with a man who thought I was much younger than I was and dumped me when the truth came out. I said in a determined voice, "Jack, I'm through with men." Jack was aghast and said, "You are too beautiful and fabulous [anybody who spent time with Jack would know that *fabulous* was one of his favourite words] to be without a partner."

While I vehemently protested any matchmaking attempts, Jack was absorbed in deep thought. Suddenly he sat up straight and I practically saw a cartoon light bulb go on over his head as he said perkily, "I know just the guy for you. He is the executive director of the White Ribbon Campaign and a good friend." And he added mischievously, "I was just at the gym with him. He works out a lot and was looking pretty good." I said no way, but he kept the pressure on me all the way home in a cab. As he walked me to my door, I finally capitulated. I agreed to go along with the idea, but only if he didn't tell his friend what was happening. He happily hopped back in the cab saying, "I can't wait to tell Olivia."

Jack kept his word. There was a party at his house in February and he called to let me know that the man in question would be present and I must come. I showed up at the appointed hour. Jack pointed out this handsome dude leaning against a wall and nervously asked me what I thought. I said I thought he looked pretty good and I would be at least willing to meet him. Jack introduced us and even thought-fully put on slow music so we could dance up close.

The rest is history. Richard and I have been together for fourteen years and we were fortunate to have Jack as best man at our wedding in June 2009. He cycled over to City Hall in the rain and, although very dapper, he was a little damp as he stood with us and my daughter Astra throughout the cere-mony, looking for all the world like a proud father. He and Olivia came to the wedding party at our house later that after-noon and Jack was one of the last ones to leave. He was clearly having a marvellous time because he was surrounded by many old and dear friends. Bringing two of his best friends together was something about which Jack was very proud and one of his favourite successful projects that he liked to boast about.

The Canyons of the Nahanni
NEIL HARTLING

Most photos of Jack portray a handsome, dapper, business-suited man. I knew another Jack.

The Nahanni is a fabled river in the Northwest Territories, encompassing Canada's deepest river canyons and a water-fall, Virginia Falls, nearly twice the height of Niagara—truly a dramatic symbol of Canadian wilderness. In 2007, the decade-long campaign to protect the entire Nahanni water-shed was in full swing and desperately needed high-profile supporters to drive the message home. Jack and Olivia took up the cause. I met them on a week-long Nahanni expedition that I was guiding at that crucial juncture of the campaign.

In spite of busy schedules, Olivia had pushed for the Nahanni trip as she is a keen whitewater canoeist. Jack was quick to throw himself into the enterprise. As a one-time near-Olympic-level swimmer, he was certainly comfortable on and in the water. I had worked with high-profile groups over the years, experiencing all manner of characters. Strong leaders are often hard to lead, but the best leaders know when it is time to follow, and these two were perfect at adjusting their roles as required. Jack and Olivia were delightful travel partners. Two indelible memories remain with me.

The first was the unique situation that Jack had arranged—to send podcasts from the expedition as part of the conservation campaign strategy. Of course there is no cell service anywhere near the Nahanni. Most consider that to be one of its attractions! So we had to rely on satellite telephones, which can be hit-and-miss at the best of times. A ritual evolved around these broadcasts. At "podcast time," Jack and Olivia would excuse themselves from camp, go off to a quiet spot in the canyons, and try to link up with the satellites. Sitting on rocks or logs, Jack would work from some scribbled key points, and in spite of the tenuous, quirky connection would deliver an inspiring message in his radio-announcer voice. Even when he had to repeat the entire production because of a lost radio connection, he was unflustered and smooth, not missing a beat. The contrast between the rustic "sound studio" and the polished words and recognizable voice of the leader of the NDP made for a humorously incongruous memory.

The mighty canyons of the Nahanni have a great parting gift for keen canoeists, and this was the location of my second recollection. Lafferty's Riffle, an understated rapid, offers a complete range of options. Stick to the left and you can skirt it completely, avoiding any waves. The farther you go to the right, the greater the rollers and the steeper the troughs between the peaks of the waves. Farthest to the right, along the canyon wall, is a bucking bronco of a ride that tests the mettle of all who venture near.

The morning sun was breaking over the canyon rim, flooding the depths with light and warmth as we approached the rapid. Jack and I were in one canoe and Olivia was in the other with her paddling partner. Drifting down the quiet stretch above that fabled rapid, we reviewed the options. "How far to the right?" I asked. "All the way," was Olivia's instant reply, followed by Jack's "Yee-haa!"

Photographer and river guide Melanie Siebert had descended ahead of us and, from the safety of an eddy, snapped a dramatic photo that captured the action and the grinning face of a man who embraced life to the fullest. That's the Jack I knew.

Community-Group Central
DAVID RAESIDE

Jack Layton helped introduce me to Toronto city politics. I began teaching at the University of Toronto in 1974, and within a few years was searching for critical and engaging material on Toronto. There wasn't much there, but two Ryerson professors, Layton and Myer Siemiatycki, had prepared a series of radio tapes on city politics. For at least a couple of years, I played excerpts to a class I taught on "power."

In 1979, I timidly involved myself in sexual-diversity politics by volunteering at *The Body Politic*, at the time one of the world's leading gay/lesbian liberation magazines. My anger at the massive 1981 police raids on several gay bathhouses was the catalyst for more substantial involvement with the Right to Privacy Committee (RTPC), the lead group taking up the charge against anti-gay police attacks. In 1982 I also joined the Citizens' Independent Review of Police Activities (CIRPA), in large part as an RTPC representative, and a year later I was the group's secretary.

Jack was first elected to City Council in 1982, joining such forceful reformers as John Sewell and Richard Gilbert. Almost immediately after first being elected, he allowed his small office to serve as a base for community groups, CIRPA among them. When he was in, he seemed the centre of a swirl of activists, and apart from two not-very-large desks most of the space was consumed by boxes of files spilling out into the corridor.

The CIRPA committee itself drew together prominent leftist lawyers, representatives of the black and Asian communities, civil libertarians, and seasoned civic activists such as Allan Sparrow, who had formed the group in 1981 after serving a stint as a city councillor. Several of the group's key members knew a great deal about police operations, as well as police prejudices. Its approach was both confrontational and co-operative—a blend that embodied Jack's approach to politics. Jack wasn't typically at meetings, but we all knew that he instinctively understood the need to change the way the city was policed, and having that base in the heart of City Hall was a huge advantage for CIRPA, enabling a great deal of its work to take place there. His political optimism was also an incentive to keep going.

The centrality of Jack's office for community groups was in full evidence during the distribution of awards for local activism hosted by Layton and fellow reformer Dale Martin around 1984 or 1985. The array of groups and causes was astounding, and almost everyone in that large City Hall lounge would have said that Jack's help was crucial.

The energies of CIRPA's key players went elsewhere by

mid-decade, but there was no question of Layton's continuing commitment to change. There was also never a shred of doubt about his support for LGBT causes. I remember him auctioneering regularly for fundraisers, squeezing more money out of a crowd than I would have thought possible. He helped shift the city towards action on AIDS that same decade, significantly before the federal government and most provincial governments took the epidemic seriously. He was in Pride parades before it was politically popular to march.

Jack became a leader among reformist councillors during the 1980s, a time when the mayoralty was in the hands of the blandly unremarkable Art Eggleton. Forceful advocacy from council members on all aspects of diversity and policing were essential to shaking off political complacency and giving voice to the marginalized.

Two Snapshots
BILL FREEMAN

One: I was with Olivia and a group of others in their Huron Street home talking about organizing in the coming election. Jack suddenly came through the back door with three or four of his young political staff. They had just flown in from the west coast and they all looked tired. I had never seen Jack look so exhausted, but he called out, "Olivia, is there anything to eat in the house? These people are famished." That was Jack.

Two: I was with a group of Toronto Island residents who met him early one morning in his office to strategize about trying to find a way to persuade Metro to finally settle the "Save Island Homes" issue. It was the first time I had met him, but he already knew who I was and how I fit into the Island. There was no small talk. Jack had another meeting and his time was short. He helped our group hammer out our objectives and gave us suggestions on our strategy. Before he rushed off he typed up a memo on his computer listing the decisions we had made, printed it off, gave it to us, and then hurried out of the room. That, too, was Jack.

Feeding the City
DEBBIE FIELD

Jack was one of the first Canadian politicians and social-movement leaders to understand the importance of the food movement. The important food policies he was responsible for championing were among his many great accomplishments. Jack also loved food—all kinds of food, but especially healthy local food and the food cooked by Olivia's mom, Ho Sze Chow. Food was always a part of any visit to Jack and Olivia's home, and Jack's enjoyment of life was evident in his enjoyment of good food.

In 1985, when hunger was becoming a serious problem in Toronto and FoodShare was created by Mayor Art Eggleton as a response to anti-hunger activists such as Rev. Stuart Coles, Jack was right there. We have a picture in the FoodShare archives from those years, showing Jack with then-Toronto Councillor Chris Korwin-Kuczynski, Sheila White, and another colleague at an early food drive at City Hall.

In 1989, on the recommendation of his friend and executive assistant, the late Dan Leckie, Jack brought Tim Lang from England to explain the value of food-policy councils. As Wayne Roberts described in his tribute to Jack in *NOW* magazine, Jack was responsible for the creation of the Toronto Food Policy Council (TFPC), the first food-policy council in North America, which hired Rod MacRae in 1991 as its first coordinator. The TFPC has now celebrated its twentieth anniversary.

Jack was also right there when parent activists like myself wanted the city, boards of education, and community organizations to help create student-nutrition programs. Rereading Jack's 1991 letter shows his amazing vision and his understanding of the power of food, his optimistic excitement for creative solutions, and the way he could mobilize and cut through jurisdictional barriers to create solutions:

> *This program is a collective community response emphasizing community control and participation to the deep local health concern about nutrition. In the process it also encourages community development. It addresses in a dignified way problems of hunger and it will have major preventative and environmental benefits. I hope we can convince all levels of government to be a part.*

On food issues, and especially on student nutrition, the Jack Layton–Olivia Chow partnership was always evident. Olivia's years as a school trustee made her the leading Canadian promoter of student nutrition, and she was the first federal politician to call for a national student-nutrition policy. Jack was always there to support Olivia's initiatives, negotiating deals with Mayor Mel Lastman and persuading many that the health of the children of Toronto was important to the city, even if some thought student nutrition was a "provincial" education matter. Olivia and Jack's traditions live on at the City of Toronto, where the great importance of student nutrition was manifest in the summer of 2011 in huge numbers of deputations defending city funding of programs.

Jack was also visionary in his recognition of the importance of community gardens, city funding for food programs, and the tremendous role that food programs play in building community. After his successes on housing, Jack turned his attention to food. He developed the idea of the Food and Hunger Action Committee, which eventually resulted in the creation of city food-program grants, and FoodShare's Animator program, which facilitates community gardens, kitchens, and markets in low-income neighbourhoods, thereby building access to food and stronger communities citywide.

Throughout all these years, Jack and Olivia have been supporters of FoodShare. During the SARS crisis, they suggested to the Barenaked Ladies that they donate a portion of their concert proceeds to FoodShare. And when we asked for a recipe for an upcoming FoodShare cookbook, the pair sent us both Olivia's mom's apple-and-pear drink recipe—which she said "is good for people who use their throats a lot"—and Jack's treasured bouillabaisse recipe.

I had the great pleasure of working with Jack before I came to FoodShare. When I worked at the Development Education Centre in the 1980s, we often needed help from the city and found our way to the offices of Jack Layton and Dale Martin, the two downtown city councillors who were responsible for so many good things that happened in the city in those days. I actually did not know the difference between Jack and Dale for years, often getting them mixed up! On some level it did not matter whom you ended up seeing when you went down to City Hall, Jack or Dale: either would respond to a community problem and come up with a solution that could help.

I went to work at City Hall as Dale's executive assistant in 1988. Together, Jack, Dale, Dan Leckie, and I, along with others on the progressive side of Council, contributed to the idea—articulated by Dan—of being "propositional" rather than "oppositional." Heavily influenced by John Sewell and the municipal reformers who preceded us but equally influenced by social movements, we were part of a movement that wanted to get things done. Disarmament, environment, women's rights, gay liberation, third-world solidarity, and anti-poverty movements were legitimate players in a complex partnership of activists in and outside government. Years later, after Luiz Inácio Lula da Silva was elected president of Brazil, Jack was interested in my proposition that we could benefit in Canada from modelling Lula's view that the Partido dos Trabalhadores (Workers' Party of Brazil) stood on two legs— the social movements and the elected party politicians.

I think much of Jack's success was that he understood this so well. When he stood up in the House of Commons, as years earlier he had stood up at City Hall, he was speaking on behalf of mobilized people in social movements. He could then convince Mel Lastman or Stephen Harper why legislative or policy change was needed. Although his main forum of activity for many of the past years has been Parliament, there is no politician in Canada who showed greater respect for grassroots activists.

When Jack decided to move to federal politics and run for the leadership of the NDP, there was some feeling that he had no chance of winning. After all, he was from Toronto, was not even an MP, and perhaps was more on the social-movement side than the electoral side of the NDP. I was pleased to play a small part in encouraging activists in social movements to get involved, launching "Give Jack a Hand," a campaign in some ways based on the community development model of FoodShare's Good Food Box. We each asked ten people we knew to support Jack, and they each asked ten—and so on and so on.

Speaking to a group of Jack supporters that year, I suggested that in politics, "every once in a while the sun breaks through the clouds and a new direction is possible." Under Jack Layton's leadership, the sun did break through the clouds. He moved mountains with his great willpower, vision, humility, and passion. When I've watched Stephen Harper recently, it has almost seemed that Jack's attitudes about partnerships and compromise and ability to "rise above" may have rubbed off a bit on the prime minster, as he speaks more of consensus building.

Jack brought out the best in all of us, and that is why he is so loved. He gave us all hope that we could rise to the occasion and make Canada a better place. For all of us in the food movement Jack Layton leaves a powerful vision of the importance of food in every single Canadian's life, a legacy of strong policy initiatives, and a can-do attitude. Jack's message to us could not be clearer. We have a developed agenda that the vast majority of Canadians agree with and practical, doable solutions.

Get Involved
DI McINTYRE

As children, we participated in numerous activities for the Montreal Association for the Blind, serving at picnic outings, participating in singsongs and bingo games at Cheerio Club (organized by our grandmother for people who were otherwise shut in), scoring for bowling teams, and volunteering endless hours in fundraising efforts. Our parents set good examples, participating actively in their communities as leaders of youth groups, choirs, and community associations, and in community activism. Encouragement to get involved was often presented to us as "Here is an opportunity for you to serve." We were also told that nothing was impossible if you are determined and willing to work towards a goal and that we should live as we wished to be remembered.

Jack did. He believed that together we can change the world, and that when you believe in something you should take action, get involved, and support those who are leading. When faced with unfairness or wrongdoing, many are silent, but if just one person has the courage to speak out, others often come forward. In his book *Speaking Out Louder: Ideas that Work for Canadians*, Jack spoke about the need "to advocate for positive change. To move from opposition to proposition. To build instead of diminish."

4

A Man for the Country

Jack was never one to take the easy way. Nor was he easily discouraged. After running for mayor in 1991 and losing to June Rowlands, he decided to try something more ambitious the next time. Two years later, he ran as the federal NDP candidate in Toronto's Rosedale riding. Given that Rosedale included the traditional bastion of old Toronto money, few were surprised when he was not elected. Still undeterred, he decided to try his chances nationally again, and this time he was thinking really big: why not start at the top?

To the amazement of many, he became national NDP leader on the first ballot, and the image of what a leader should be was changed forever...although maybe not right away. A disappointing showing for the party in the 2004 election was in part due to a casual statement by Jack— impassioned but unfortunate—to the effect that Paul Martin was responsible for the deaths of homeless people because there was no national housing strategy. Jack learned from his mistakes, though, and in each subsequent election, the NDP gained ground.

On December 1, 2008, the Liberals and NDP, with the support of the Bloc, signed a coalition agreement, setting out the principles by which they would govern if the Conservatives lost the upcoming confidence vote. We may never know what arguments convinced the Governor General to agree to prorogue Parliament rather than have the government fall, but prorogue it she did. And the NDP and Jack lost an opportunity.

But by the time the next federal election rolled around in 2011, Jack and the NDP were ready. At first, many dismissed the reports of an "orange wave" sweeping across Quebec, but when the ballots were finally counted on May 2, the country learned that he had led the NDP to the largest number of seats in their history. Jack and his party now formed the Official Opposition.

"Jack, You Want to Do What?"
TERRY GRIER

In 2002, the federal New Democratic Party was demoralized and depressed. Its official party status in the House of Commons had barely survived the 2000 election. Single-issue politics on the left was eroding party loyalty; many were calling for a more actively radical kind of politics; the party's very being was being called into question. Alexa McDonough was stepping down as leader, and a new leader would be chosen in 2003 not by a delegate convention but, for the first time, by one member, one vote.

When Jack called to sound me out about his running for the leadership, I was initially surprised—it seemed quite a leap for a municipal politician. Could he walk in the same shoes as Tommy Douglas, David Lewis, Ed Broadbent? But as we talked, I came around to encouraging him. He had twice been a federal candidate in the 1990s. He had spent nineteen years on Toronto Council, where he was the respected leader of the sizeable left-leaning group of councillors. He was deputy mayor, and as president of the Federation of Canadian Municipalities he was the acknow-ledged spokesperson for Canada's cities. He was eager to take his political vision onto the national stage.

Soon he officially declared his candidacy. Not yet firmly decided, I went to a coffee party where Jack was to meet with potential supporters. As all candidates do, he spoke of rebuilding party morale, growing membership, modernizing party organization. But what impressed me was the way he spoke confidently of his chances of winning the leadership, and his well-thought-out organizational and financial plans for the contest. He believed that he would win, that the money could be raised, that the organization could be built. As in earlier years, that incredible energy and optimism leapt out at you. In the course of an hour of hard-headed back-and-forth from seasoned party workers, he persuaded us that it could be done. We were seeing a demonstration of his leadership in action. I signed on.

In late November, Ruth and I were at a fundraiser for Jack. About 450 turned up, the great majority in their thirties and forties, many new to us, others whom we hadn't seen since the Broadbent years. It was a classy event—contemporary entertainment, people obviously enjoying themselves—and it raised more than $80,000. Jack made a fine speech. I came away more than ever persuaded that he was the man for the job.

For the previous several years I had been comforting myself with the thought that the swing of the political pendulum would eventually bring the national NDP back into relevance and influence. The leader would be an important factor in this, but not everything. I had been kidding myself. If we didn't make a breakthrough the next time round, we would be for all intents and purposes finished on the national scene.

So this contest was crucial, and the key issue for me was who could best reach beyond the core 8 to 10 per cent we had been reduced to. That night I knew it had to be Jack. I saw him display a confident and affectionate familiarity with the leadership of virtually every social-reform movement in the country, a passionate and genuine desire to bring about real change, a presence on the platform that moved his audience emotionally, an impressive grasp of policy, a thoughtful sensitivity towards individuals he talked to, and a huge vitality which gave the evening an energy and exuberance I hadn't seen for a dozen years.

It became utterly clear to me now that he was far and away the best—indeed, the only one with the qualities to lift the party, to take it beyond its aging and narrowing base, to connect it with the many sane groups and individuals who didn't see formal politics as a useful way of achieving reform, to give us energy and optimism and a hope of winning.

In January 2003, Jack won the leadership on the first ballot. The following morning, honouring an earlier commitment to a student organization, he spoke to a packed audience at Ryerson. We responded, as so many would in the years ahead, to his optimistic vision, his energy, his profound decency. With Jack, we were feeling good about the future.

The NDP's new leader was on his way.

Taking the Grassroots National
JAMEY HEATH

Ottawa was a sweat bath the day Jack Layton announced he wanted to be NDP leader back in 2002. He did so in an open-air press conference on the lawn of Parliament Hill. And after the formalities were done, we returned to my modest, air-conditioning-free apartment a few blocks from the Hill so he could do a long list of interviews.

Most of these were done semi-nude, I discovered as I glanced up to see most of Jack's clothes piled on my couch and him holding court, phone in hand, on my balcony. Looking back, it's fitting his lack of airs were on such full display: he was the real deal, an opinion which many Canadians of all walks of life clearly shared.

I didn't know him when I first joined his leadership campaign. But as we were preparing for that first press conference, he insisted that a group of housing activists from Quebec be there. (He had worked with them while he was president of the Federation of Canadian Municipalities, with some success.) This, it should be said, was less than ideal. The launch was already a bit of a circus. Adding more people seemed unwise.

To Jack, however, the housing activists were a symbol of how Canadians could get something done together—acknowledging Quebec's difference within a flexible federalism. Years later, this would manifest itself in a historic election result. But this was less a grandiose plan than core belief: if the will was there to work together, a way could be found.

Although it's difficult now to remember a time when Jack wasn't a household figure, the day he launched his leadership campaign one reporter asked me who he was. After I pointed him out, she cooed that he looked like Paul Newman. Others were not so kind. Experts who weren't asking why he would want to win were confidently predicting he would lose. But he would have none of it, and he set about infecting as many people as possible with his relentless optimism and faith that the fact that something hadn't happened yet didn't mean it couldn't. He won on the first ballot.

Our only fight came in a blues bar in Ottawa's ByWard Market about two days after he became leader. He asked how many seats the NDP would win in the next election. I said twenty-five, almost twice as many as the party had then, but Jack saw this as defeatism. "Think bigger," he said, before telling his favourite sports story. You might think this would involve the Montreal Canadiens, but it was actually about water polo: "Politics is like water polo. Stay calm on the surface, work underwater where they can't see you, and then kick hard."

Many politicians might think the point of kicking harder

was for their own advancement, but not Jack. And the reason, I think, why his death touched so many people wasn't just the unfairness of coming so soon after such a breakthrough. It was that people realized his smile was for real—that there was a politician out there in it for more people than himself.

I first realized this walking into his house with him once. I remember being taken aback that there was a community meeting in his living room. Jack took it in stride. As one does, he had given out keys to his house so people had a place to organize.

His belief in people and their power to change things was unshakable. Anyone and everyone could reach his BlackBerry in those early days, and most mornings their suggestions were enthusiastically passed along. If there was a problem, Jack wanted to fix it. Once, he was giving a major speech on health care. But he had just returned from a First Nations community with squalid living conditions and wanted the speech to be about that, too. It was a rambling, disjointed speech—but he didn't care. He was determined that the blue-chip audience would hear about the true misery he'd seen.

Being political staff isn't always the most rewarding of jobs: people tend to think you will say anything that reflects well on the boss. So, when asked why he was such a "used-car salesman" or why he smiled so much, my reply—that he really was like that—often met with, well, let's just call it cynicism.

In later years, many of these same people wrote how courageous Jack was, with his cane and cancer, battling through a campaign with a smile and good grace. What too few people saw until it was tragically too late was the smile and good nature were very much who he was: someone who saw the best in others and wanted to work with them.

The other thing you couldn't help noticing at Toronto

City Hall the night before his funeral was how the crowd, and the chalked messages, reflected the person they honoured. This, too, was fitting, for Jack's affection knew no barriers. A doctor from abroad driving a taxi, a blue-collar worker looking for a job, an Aboriginal community living in shacks, or a newly married gay couple—it made no difference.

Much had changed since that soupy day when he set out to change Canadian politics, more than nine years earlier. How he went about doing that will, no doubt, be scrutinized elsewhere. But from stories of his earliest days on City Council in Toronto to the final letter he wrote, through budget deals and would-be coalitions and four elections, there was one constant: Jack would work with anyone if he thought something could get done.

And while some of this was strategic politically, all of it was due to an unwavering belief in human nature and human potential to make change. So when I remember Jack, it is his human side that comes to mind first, even if the cynics didn't realize the smile was genuine until after it had really caught on. I remember the laugh after giving a speech with his neck half-cocked because one of the teleprompter screens was put on backwards. I recall the guy who carried my suitcase into the hotel for me after I'd fallen asleep on the campaign bus. And also him talking to *As It Happens*, half naked, on my balcony, the day he told the country he wanted to lead it.

An hour after Jack passed away, before the piles of flowers or acres of chalk came along, a friend texted me after getting out of an elevator. He said that people were visibly saddened, that this wasn't about another public figure but something more personal.

Of all Jack's gifts, his contagious humanity was the most precious. Fortunately, it was also the one most easily passed on.

The Rule of Three
ANNE McGRATH

Jack was full of ideas. Many of them were very good. But not all of them were helpful to the goal of electing more New Democrats and forming government. He had many people feeding him ideas, from the taxi driver to a passerby on the street to international experts on the greatest issues of the day. It didn't matter to Jack. He loved absorbing ideas and kicking them around. He saw the wisdom in everyone.

When he was travelling and had lots of thinking time, he would often develop these thoughts into full-blown plans, sometimes accompanied by an Excel spreadsheet. When Brad and I met him for dinner every week, we would review these plans and hold them up to an electoral lens.

He would explain these elaborate, detailed plans—many of which would take years and a small army to implement—with great enthusiasm. But that wasn't the exercise for him. He was a big-ideas guy and that's what people loved about him. He was optimistic in what could be achieved, but some of his big plans could just not be supported by either our resources or the timeline. We would—with respect—look at Jack with knowing glances and say, "We could do that...or...we could try and win the next tier of seats in the upcoming campaign." Fortunately, because Jack was as practical and pragmatic as he was idealistic and empathetic, he appreciated the grounding his team would offer him as part of their jobs.

Those who knew Jack well before he became federal leader passed on a very helpful piece of advice about how to manage his surplus of ideas. They recommended that we use the Rule of Three. When Jack had an idea that we judged either unmanageable, too expensive, too time consuming, politically problematic, or just plain goofy, we would ignore it the first time, and then the second time, and wait for the third request. He knew that not all of his ideas were perfect, and he accepted that there had to be a filter. He actually appreciated the effort—but he was also on to us. In the last year, when he really wanted something done, he would say, "This is the third time I've asked about this. I know about the Rule of Three, and I really want this to happen." It was always said with firmness, and a twinkle in his eye.

Working It Out
NANCY LAYTON

Jack moved to Toronto to do graduate studies at York in the early 1970s while I stayed in Montreal to start a career in education. As is probably typical of many siblings who move apart, we saw each other at family occasions and kept in touch with the odd phone call, but we were both occupied with our own lives.

This changed when Jack asked me to travel with him during the 2008 federal election campaign. I was to be his "personal assistant"—not quite as important as it might sound. With his wife, Olivia Chow, campaigning for her own seat, Jack needed someone to look after the nonpolitical side of things: his clothing and luggage, his meals, and so on. It was a fun experience, if somewhat exhausting: the days were long, the nights too short, and Jack kept adding another guitar to his collection on the plane. Jack seemed to appreciate having a family member along even if we didn't have that much time to spend together.

In the months afterward, Jack would often call while en

route to an event or waiting in an airport (but only after he had called our mom). He enjoyed sharing the daily ups and downs of his life in Ottawa and always wanted to have news of our lives in the Eastern Townships.

In February 2011, with an election appearing likely, Jack once again asked me to be his PA and I agreed. Little did I know at the time that I would be playing a much more significant role, as just before the election call Jack underwent hip surgery. As I had taught physical education for more than twenty years, he wanted me to oversee the physiotherapy required for a full recovery.

Jack and I spent an hour every day in the gym. This was most often the fitness room in a hotel, although we visited several YMCAs and in Thunder Bay Jack was honoured to be invited to use the brand-new local RCMP facility. At first, the routine was basically stretching and strengthening, but about ten days in, the physiotherapist joined us and allowed Jack to get on an elliptical machine for the first time—Jack was very emotional as he finally could do "cardio" again. During the workouts Jack and I talked, perhaps making up for all those years when we hadn't had the opportunity. We shared memories of growing up, of our parents, brothers, and families. As the campaign unfolded, we also marvelled at Canadians' response to Jack and his message.

On election night, after celebrating the unprecedented results for the NDP, Jack and I returned to the hotel. Both of us were delighted to know that by the end of the campaign, the cane had become a prop, not a necessity. As we had for the previous forty nights, we shared a good-night hug. I will always enjoy the memories of being with Jack during his remarkable rise to leader of the Official Opposition, but I cherish those hugs. Thanks, big brother.

Music in the Air
JOE MIHEVC

I remember the very first barbecue that was organized after Jack announced that he was running for leader in 2002: it was at my house. I wanted it to be a great event, and so I invited Padre Hernan Astudillo to come and play some Latin American music. Jack was a part of the Latin American community, and the Latin American community was a part of Jack, as he supported human-rights work in the 1980s and 1990s during the worst violations in Latin America.

Astudillo brought a full band and a dance troupe as well. Our backyard was totally full. Music and dance were in the air. Someone told me that they signed up over two hundred memberships that day, the largest number in the whole campaign.

Campaigning on the Rock
MARILYN CHURLEY

I grew up in Newfoundland and Labrador and was lucky to be in St. John's on several occasions when Jack was also there. The time I remember most fondly was during the NDP leadership race in 2003. I was then the deputy leader of the Ontario NDP and co-chair of Jack's national leadership campaign; consequently I was using my influence wherever I could to garner support for him.

In the early days of the campaign we had a steep hill to climb. I had lots of friends in Newfoundland and Labrador, two of whom were Bruce Pearce and Shawn Silver, who were spearheading his NL campaign. Another friend was

Jack Harris, then the leader of the provincial NDP. Although Harris was supporting Bill Blaikie for the leadership, he agreed to hold a garden party for Layton in his backyard, where he very graciously introduced him to a large crowd. I think this says a lot about Jack Harris's decency and fair-mindedness, as well as about Jack Layton's affability and ability to charm his way into anything! After the event, we took Jack to the Ship Inn, a pub on Duckworth Street, and listened to great local music. I don't know if my memory serves me right on this, but I believe much later we bar-hopped along the famous George Street and in one of the bars Jack was "screeched in"—he kissed the head of a codfish and downed a tumbler of screech.

One Renfrew Avenue
DI McINTYRE

For the seven years that my cousin Jack lived in my house in Ottawa, he called it "the NDP Stornoway." After he was chosen leader of the NDP in 2003, Jack needed somewhere to live within easy cycling distance of Parliament Hill. After I had checked out several apartments and we had gone to see a few he asked if he could move in here and "have [his] dad's old room." (Hon. Robert E. J. Layton—Uncle Bob, my godfather—had lived here during his last term as Conservative MP, before retiring from public life.) I was delighted to have Jack move in, as that gave me a unique opportunity to see him fairly often despite his very busy schedule.

Jack was very easy to live with—always positive, always appreciative of the comforts of home. The house provided a quiet retreat from his busy days. Most days he'd leave early for an interview or for meetings, riding away on his bicycle or being whisked away by a favourite taxi driver. We seldom had much conversation in the morning as he was usually engaged with his BlackBerry or in early-morning telephone meetings or interviews. Most days he squeezed in enough time to sit down at the dining-room table briefly for a strong mug of coffee and a bowl of fresh fruit salad with yogurt, and sometimes a little granola. He always thanked me for serving him breakfast, often saying, "Cuz, you don't need to get up to do this for me." I can't count the number of times he remarked, "You make the best fruit salad in Canada" or the "best coffee."

The only special furniture requests that Jack made were a desk and a piano keyboard in his bedroom. He sometimes found time to play the keyboard, but I don't think he used that desk very often, as he had so few hours at home.

When Jack did arrive home before the wee hours, he'd head straight to the kitchen and open the fridge to see what was on offer. Jack enjoyed homemade soups, especially soups made by AhMa—Ho Sze Chow, Olivia's mom. I often had a big pot of soup simmering, which he enjoyed for a late-night snack or for breakfast. Jack also enjoyed peanut butter by the tablespoon, so it became a regular pantry item. A supply of Smithwick's, one of his favourite beers, was always in the fridge.

Occasionally we'd have a chance to exchange family news, relaxing in front of the fireplace, usually with a glass of wine or a cold beer. Sometimes he'd strum on a guitar and I'd be treated to a preview of a song being readied for the press gallery dinner the next night. We shared a fairly quiet household in Ottawa during the week; then he'd spend weekends at home in Toronto or travelling across the country.

It bugged me when the press tried to belittle Jack by pinning him with the simplistic label of "Smiling Jack," as if there was something wrong with his outlook on life. Jack was a man who smiled from the inside—it was not for show, it was who he was, through and through. Jack was always optimistic, never complaining, always interested in different perspectives and responsive to ideas. In all the years he lived with me I never heard him say a bad word about anyone. He may not have liked their ideas, but always seemed to find something to like about the person. If only we could clone Jack Layton and sprinkle the world with his love of all it has to offer!

When Jack had been here for a couple of years, my daughter Leia returned to live at home after a couple of gap years abroad. Leia had always liked Jack and he seemed to delight in having academic exchanges with her on the wide range of topics she was exploring as part of her Carleton University humanities program. One night their discussion was particularly animated, as Leia had been reading Charles Taylor and was in awe that Professor Taylor had been Jack's thesis advisor at McGill.

Every night Jack would call his confidante and soulmate, Olivia, and they'd share information about their days and shared projects. The conversations always seemed to end with a few words in Cantonese. When Jack was in Ottawa and Olivia was a city councillor in Toronto, he often commented how much he missed her. Needless to say, he was delighted when she was elected to Parliament.

I began a new search for an apartment for them, but was very pleased when they asked if we could find a way that they could stay on here. We repainted the master bedroom in

Olivia's choice of deep cadmium yellow, and for three years Olivia and Jack shared my house, with two bikes now cycling to the Hill on sunny days.

After the Ottawa bus strike of 2008–9, when it had become very difficult to get taxis, Jack and Olivia decided to get an apartment closer to Parliament Hill so that they would not have to rely on others for transportation to work and would have easier access to the airport. It was the right decision, but I missed them.

My Seatmate, Jack
LIBBY DAVIES

The House of Commons is a peculiar place. The image of 308 legislators sitting at wooden desks with flip-top lids, reminiscent of an old school room, with two people per unit, row after row, engaged in a battle of words with neither side giving way, is something that visitors routinely see from the public galleries above the floor of the House of Commons. Visitors are required to pick up a telephone-type device to hear the harangue taking place below.

You could say Question Period unfolds the same way every sitting day of the House: forty-five minutes of the Opposition grilling the Government, and ministers doing anything and everything to not answer the questions asked. There is a grinding, routine element to it, certainly, but the intensity of those forty-five minutes and the amount of preparation and attention to detail reveal its importance in Canadian politics. There's a lot riding on your performance in the House and we can be merciless in our judgement of one another, notwithstanding scrutiny from the media.

As Jack Layton's House leader and deputy leader, I was his seatmate for eight years, and although I had known him for twenty years before that it gave me an uncommon perspective on who he was and what he was like. I remember Jack's first question in Question Period. It was on October 6, 2004, when he rose as the newly elected member of Parliament for Toronto–Danforth. His question zeroed in on the urgency of the climate-change crisis, emphasizing the broken promises and lack of action of the then-Liberal government. He was nervous, but not visibly so, and his question was credible and well put. I remember feeling nervous too. Sitting on his left side, I became very familiar with his stance from behind, as he turned slightly to his right side to face the government and Speaker.

Over the years, and more than 1,500 questions later, those forty-five minutes became windows for me into how he was feeling and what he was thinking. No matter what was going on he always paid attention to Olivia, who sat across from us. He listened intently to her questions and always said with pride how hard she worked her critic file. I remember the time he asked me if I thought it would be too much to wish Olivia a happy birthday in the House. Not a good time to do it, I politely replied. He didn't.

I saw his suits hang on him when he lost weight, and saw how hard it was sometimes for him to stand when he was in pain, though his face never showed it. He always propped one foot up on the shelf under his desk and neatly lined up his pen and papers on the sloping surface. He always asked for water, "no ice," and was warm and friendly to the pages and anyone who came by. He'd sign photos, books, and mementoes for folks (especially MP Carol Hughes, who even provided a special pen for him to use). His meticulous need for detail in regard to voting and what was going on in the House meant I had to be ready at all times for what he might ask. He loathed heckling, no matter which side of the House it came from. He'd sometimes mutter, "I can't hear their replies. Tell our folks to be quiet," and I'd do my best to quiet "the boys" on our side and raise the heckling issue at the House leader's meetings.

I learned not to talk to him before his questions, as he would quietly run through his lines, especially in French; but he always said hello and smiled, no matter how rough the day. After his questions we would have brief, multiple, thirty-second conversations, one ear still on what was going on in the House as we exchanged relevant information: who was doing what, what problems there were, and what we needed to do to follow up. He would often direct me to pursue a particular matter before he left to go to the scrums after Question Period. We also talked about personal things, and I came to understand that he had an enormous capacity to retain information. Anything relevant he popped in his BlackBerry notes section and he could retrieve all manner of interesting information from his precious "BB." We also joked around; whenever I swore and then said I'm sorry, he'd always say, "Never mind" with a big grin.

Over the years his questions and debate in the House took on greater depth, and became more polished and in his own voice: you could see the great capacity he had to lead government one day. When he spoke we all listened, not because we had to but because we knew he was speaking to us and all Canadians with realism, hope, and conviction. Some of his best speeches were to his caucus, behind closed doors. Jack was an incredible team builder and his ability to reach out to his caucus and bring us together, especially during difficult times, was a real hallmark of his leadership style. He always said his caucus was part of his extended family.

I recall three examples in the House, among many, that show his personality and strength.

On the lighter side was his famous "cancel the subsidies to big oil, big ass, uh, big gas" comment in 2006, which caused a hilarious uproar in the House. (The prime minister took up the slip, if not the question, with gusto, replying that he would "get to the bottom of it.") Jack sat down, saying, "I can't believe I said that," and I realized he wasn't laughing at all, even though everyone else was. I told him it was very cute and people would love it. "Okay," he said somewhat sceptically, but of course it turned out to be a turn of phrase that people loved and laughed about with affection.

In 2008, we were part of a truly historic day in the House. On June 11 the Government of Canada issued an official apology to students of residential schools. Jack had worked tirelessly for a year and half to help bring about the historic apology. He also suggested a successful way out of a strict procedural House rule that would have prevented leaders of First Nations, Inuit, and Métis from being present on the floor of the House of Commons to reply to the apology.

I believe Jack's speech that day in Parliament was a turning point. He was no longer the scrappy leader of the fourth party; he was a leader for all Canadians, who could bring us forward from a shameful history of racism and colonialism. His speech was heartfelt and important, but it was the work he had done leading up to that speech, building important relationships with Aboriginal people and understanding the issue from their point of view, that gave it weight and meaning for them. He said:

As we speak here today, thousands of Aboriginal children are without proper schools or clean water, adequate food, their own bed, good health care, safety, comfort, land, and rights. We can no longer throw our hands up in horror and say, "There's nothing we can do." Taking responsibility and working towards reconciliation means saying, "We must act together to resolve this."

That day in the House we saw our leader's ability to speak powerfully and directly to people. He was in his element, using the institutions of democratic governance to bring us closer to social justice.

On many occasions Jack used his humour and personal warmth to make a connection with people. In June 2011, during the lengthy filibuster debate on the back-to-work legislation directed at postal workers locked out by Canada Post, Jack inspired his brand-new 103-member Official Opposition caucus to take on the debate with fierceness and passion. He spoke—we all spoke, for fifty-eight long hours. Even then, as the evening wore on and he was tired and no doubt in pain, he found humour and compassion. "Are we allowed to sing?" he asked the Speaker and those in the chamber. "I imagine at times it might improve the tone of the debate." We all cracked up and cheered him on.

Jack's love for Parliament reflected both his personal history with the place and his pride in his father's work there before him. One of my favourite memories is of walking along one of the marble corridors on the sixth floor of the Centre Block near his office. Surprisingly, these corridors can be very quiet and are often deserted, even in such a busy building. With no one in sight, I heard someone around the corner whistling in a very tuneful way. As I approached the corner, there was Jack, all by himself, merrily whistling as if he had not a care in the world. We laughed and chatted for a few minutes; then off he went.

I only wish I could remember his tune.

Guns and Votes
DICK PROCTOR

"I need six votes and have no idea where I'm going to find them."

It was a gorgeous Friday afternoon in late August 2010, and Jack Layton and I were sitting in his backyard in Toronto discussing the long-gun registry and the Conservative government's announcement that it intended to hold another vote to abolish it. Liberal leader Michael Ignatieff had announced that the whips were on for his caucus to vote unanimously to keep the registry. The Bloc Québécois MPs would also vote unanimously to maintain the registry, reflecting Quebec voters' enthusiastic support for it. It was the December 6, 1989, Montreal massacre of fourteen female students at the École Polytechnique that had precipitated the passage of Bill C-68 establishing the registry.

With fewer than half the seats in the House of Commons, the Conservatives couldn't eliminate the registry alone. With the Liberals and BQ unanimously opposed, obviously the six votes the Conservatives still needed would have to come from members of the fourth party in Parliament— the NDP. This was something the NDP leader desperately wanted to prevent. Jack had been a co-founder of the White Ribbon Campaign to eliminate violence against women and recognized that maintaining a long-gun registry was an important element in achieving that goal. He also clearly had his eye on the next election and knew that any NDP support to allow the Conservatives to repeal the registry would be viewed negatively. He had already persuaded three MPs to switch their vote on the issue. Finding six more would be extremely difficult.

Adding to Jack's difficulty was that MPs would be voting on a private member's bill, C-391. Traditionally, all political parties have viewed private member's bills as an opportunity for each MP to vote his or her conscience on the proposed legislation. In this instance, the Liberals had suspended that tradition. Groups and individuals who supported keeping the registry congratulated Liberal leader Michael Ignatieff for his wisdom in whipping the Liberal vote, and criticized Jack Layton for failing to do likewise. To thwart the Conservatives' desire to kill the registry would require all of the NDP leader's charm, energy, enthusiasm, and ability with members of his own caucus.

The long-gun registry had been an election issue in rural Canada in every federal election since 1995. Despite six policy conventions in the intervening fifteen years and the accusation from our political opponents that our party has a position on everything, the NDP had been unable to come up with a uniform policy on the long-gun registry. This inability stemmed from the fact that NDP MPs from rural areas generally reflected their constituents' views that the legislation was aimed squarely at them, all, naturally, law-abiding citizens. Rural constituents argued that the gang violence and murders in Canada's largest cities were not the fault of rural gun owners; yet it was the gun owners who were being forced to pay to register their long guns, so the impact of the legislation was borne unfairly by them.

There were also the huge cost overruns that plagued the registry. This occurred because Jean Chrétien's Liberal government had refused to force provincial and territorial governments to administer the long-gun registry in each jurisdiction. In every federal election campaign after 1995, signs appeared on rural yards throughout Canada urging voters to "Remember C-68." By contrast, gun control was not a vote-determining issue for the vast majority of people living in urban areas. More women supported the registry than men, but that was also true in rural Canada. When most urban Canadians marked their ballots, the candidate or party's position on the long-gun registry was not uppermost in their mind.

Because the NDP lacked a clear, coherent position on C-68, NDP candidates running for nominations in rural areas had been emboldened, and some ran on the promise, "Elect me and I'll vote to kill the gun registry." Some had been elected to Parliament, and it would be next to impossible for Jack to convince those MPs to climb down from the horse they'd won on. How, under such circumstances, could he possibly find the votes needed to keep the registry?

Jack had something going for him that I had never witnessed in a lifetime of political activity. He categorically refused—publicly or privately—ever to badmouth a political friend. He would disagree with their position, but never make it personal. In the rough-and-tumble of political life, Jack's approach was simply extraordinary—mocking the old refrain that the difference between a cactus and a caucus is that, with a cactus, the pricks are all on the outside! Because of this approach, as well as all his innate leadership talents and abilities, he was respected by all caucus members and beloved by the vast majority of them.

I watched from afar over the next few weeks as Jack met with the full caucus prior to the reopening of Parliament. The media reported that additional rural NDP members were now leaning towards supporting the registry. Suddenly, Canadians learned that Jack needed to find only one more MP and the Conservative motion would be lost. One long-shot possibility was Peter Stoffer, who had represented a rural area outside Halifax since 1997. Peter squeaked in that year on a recount but continued to pile up larger and larger pluralities in succeeding campaigns. His mantra: "Knock on 600 doors a day during an election and you'll win."

One of Peter's unique techniques, when in Ottawa, is to cold-call constituents at home: "Good evening Mrs. Jones, this is Peter Stoffer, your member of Parliament. I'm call-ing to see if there are any federal issues you care to discuss with me." One can only imagine the positive impact for Mr. Stoffer's reputation when Mrs. Jones relayed that story to her coworkers the following day. Peter was also the perennial Congeniality Award winner for the most-liked MP by peers on all sides of the House. When it came to the long-gun registry Peter Stoffer had been consistent. Each and every time it came up for a vote in the House between 1997 and 2010, Peter had voted to kill it. He said that was what his constituents wanted, and his constituents were never wrong.

Peter was the caucus defence critic when Jack was elected leader in 2003 and, early on, there was a controversy between them that was so skilfully handled that most caucus members were unaware of it. Peter and Jack had taken different positions publicly on a defence-policy issue and, when a reporter pointed this out, Peter replied, "Jack's new. He'll learn." On reading Stoffer's quote, Jack called him into his office and stripped him of his defence-critic position. Next, Jack made several critic changes simultaneously so that Peter's loss of the defence portfolio was never apparent to the rest of caucus. Still, a political confrontation such as this would usually result in a lack of confidence, trust, and goodwill between the two that would not be easily over-come. To both of their credit, together with Jack's refusal ever to be negative, they repaired their relationship.

Now, seven years later, here was Peter Stoffer saying he'd just seen a poll of his constituents showing a majority now supported keeping the long-gun registry. He would respect their wishes. Bill C-391 was defeated on September 22, 2010. But after winning a majority in May 2011, the Conservatives moved quickly to abolish the long-gun regis-try. Had all Jack's work been in vain?

Jack told me something else in his backyard that after-noon that made everything else pale by comparison. His doctors had advised him that he had a virulent form of pros-tate cancer, similar to the strain that had killed his father. "I won't see my granddaughter Beatrice grow up. I won't live to see seventy," he said. (He would tell me in January 2011 that the doctors had advised him that they now had the prostate cancer under control, a point he reiterated at his final news conference on July 25, 2011, when he said he was dealing with a new form of cancer.)

Five days after the orange wave in Quebec had dramat-ically propelled Jack to leader of Her Majesty's Loyal Opposition I accompanied him to Regina for the memorial service of former Saskatchewan Premier Allan Blakeney. During the trip, Jack linked the historic breakthrough in Quebec with the gun-control vote the previous September. "We won fifty-nine seats in Quebec on Monday. If we'd voted to abolish the gun registry last fall, we'd have been lucky to win one seat in that province," he said.

Listening to the soaring oratory of Stephen Lewis and Rev. Brent Hawkes at Jack's state funeral on August 27, 2011, and knowing how much I loved and would miss this sparkling, kind, and thoughtful man, I was struck by the realization that our conversation in his backyard had occurred exactly one year earlier, to the very hour.

A Kyoto Plan
PETER TABUNS

Shortly after the 2004 election, Jack hired me as his climate-change advisor. He wanted to put together a Kyoto plan for the NDP. My job was to draft a plan showing that Canada could do it, and could afford to do it. Thus started an intense process to move the agenda on an issue that was central for him, even while he was finding his feet on Parliament Hill and building an organization for the next election.

We would meet every week to review progress and to discuss problems that had cropped up. It was common for him to start his round of meetings at 7:30 AM or earlier; around 10 PM he would come to my office, pick up his bicycle, and walk it down Bank Street between piles of snow as we reviewed what we had found and what the Liberal government was doing (or not doing) to meet Canada's Kyoto commitments. Despite his overflowing plate he kept track of all the details: he remembered off the top of his head what had happened in earlier meetings and what needed detailed follow-up. He had been working on climate issues for close to two decades and knew both the policy issues and the urgency of the task.

It was during those late-night walks that he would make clear what he felt the country needed to do and what we as a party needed to do to move thinking away from the dangerous path Canada was on. For someone who was still a new leader it was impressive that this issue was so high on his list of urgent concerns.

Taking the Time
MICHAEL GOLDRICK

With our local NDP candidate, I attended a rally for Jack just days before the 2011 election. I hadn't seen Jack for quite a while and I wanted to contact him to wish him well and to have him do a publicity photograph with our candidate. Well, the rally was immense, excitement was high, and Jack was in top oratorical gear. I have to say that I was a little hesitant to take up his time for the unscheduled photo op, but in true Layton form, he did the shoot and then took ten precious minutes to catch up with me.

It was not until later that I came to realize that at the time he was suffering considerable pain. Yet despite that, he had just delivered a "barn-burner" and taken the time to connect with our candidate and with me. It was those sorts of attributes that made Jack such an admirable person, and a good and constant friend. Unpretentious, ambitious certainly, but generous and caring both to his friends and to "ordinary" people.

The "Project"
PAUL MOIST

Jack Layton and I assumed our respective leadership positions in 2003: he became federal NDP leader in January, and I became CUPE's national president in November of that same year. My friendship with Jack developed over the years we shared as leaders of our organizations. But I did not realize back in 2003 what a profound impact he would have on my life, my activism, and my leadership.

I knew Jack from a distance through his municipal career in Toronto. Then we had a lengthy chat—the first of many—on a beautiful June day in 2002 after he had dropped by our Western Municipal Workers Conference in Regina. He approached me at the conference saying we needed to chat. He wanted to talk about "the project," a term I would hear repeatedly for the next nine years. He said he knew I was running for CUPE's national presidency, knew of my municipal career, and assumed I would be supporting Bill Blaikie, given my Manitoba roots.

For the next couple of hours over a couple of beers, he described his plans to secure strong municipal activists to run, and to commit to running in at least two elections. He spoke passionately about the necessity and viability of our party making its long-awaited breakthrough in Quebec and of the important role CUPE could play in building our party. He was thoughtful, erudite, funny, and full of plans. And, as I recall, he barely took a breath. We exchanged particulars and promised to keep in touch. Little did I know what this meant when it came to Jack, but I was about to learn.

In November of that year, he spoke to our national convention in Quebec City. On the stage, he whispered to me that we had to get together—he had something that he had to discuss. We met later that month and he outlined his plans for fundraising until the end of the year, when new rules would limit union and corporate donations to federal political parties. This part of the "project" involved raising enough capital to purchase a building in Ottawa, an asset that could both serve the party physically and become collateral for loans in future elections. Like many others, I could not say no to Jack. He got my $250,000 commitment from CUPE; I gained an agenda item to add to my first National Executive Board meeting as CUPE's presiding officer.

In 2004 and 2008 he called asking for a quick favour: could he borrow Anne McGrath, a respected member of our national staff? As these were campaign requests, they were expected to last some six weeks. On the first occasion, the loan of Anne lasted a year; on the second, his short-term request lasted for the remainder of his time as leader, as McGrath became his chief of staff. I never let him forget his "raiding" activities and how he had snookered me, again!

Communication with Jack Layton could take place any hour of the day, any day of the week. He would text or email first to confirm a time for the call. As he knew my hours, his calls took place either before 6 AM or after 11 PM. The range of issues was vast. He called to talk about the 2004 Martin budget, which the party supported after securing some $4 billion in improvements and delayed corporate tax cuts. And then it was the 2005 budget, in which I thought we might be relinquishing a national child-care program and, perhaps, needed health-care improvements. I lost that argument but still the calls kept coming.

As a longtime municipal activist and past president of the Federation of Canadian Municipalities (FCM), Jack was a popular guest speaker at the FCM's annual June convention. He and I always met for coffee, and he'd drop by our booth. At his last FCM, in Halifax, he asked that we meet in his room. When I arrived he was half dressed, but welcomed me as he put on makeup to cover his pallor. We chatted about the breakthrough he had achieved in the recent federal election. He wanted to talk about the future, about how we'd sell memberships and create party capacity and infrastructure at the riding level in Quebec.

I escorted him to the convention centre. It took a full twenty-five minutes to walk about half a block. Jack was mobbed on the way by every councillor and mayor. He had his cane and looked both thin and tired, but he had a moment for everyone, time for every picture, time to come to our booth for a photo, and time to appear before the gathering for a thunderous ovation from the more than 2,000 delegates.

My last in-person encounter with Jack was like the first, some nine years previously. I ran into him and Olivia in the Ottawa airport after the postal-workers legislation debate. He looked exhausted. He was eating a piece of pizza on a concrete bench in the departure area. I said hi but that I'd let him and Olivia have some peace to eat their quick supper. He, of course, would not hear of this. There were things to discuss, principally Quebec. In the ten minutes we were together, we were interrupted four times by people he did not know, walking over to congratulate him and wish him all the best. He made time for each of them, yet never skipped a beat in our discussion of the next phase of the "project."

I emailed Jack after his July news conference where he announced he was again battling cancer and needed to step aside to focus on it. I did not expect a reply, but as usual I was wrong:

Thanks Paul for your thoughts and support as we face the next steps in life's journey.

It is great to know we have the support of half a million public-sector workers from coast to coast.

The "project" will need everything we can muster in the tough battles that lie ahead. I have every confidence that we will continue to grow and succeed and that the vision we had will come to fruition.

Be well and take care,

Jack

Presiding over the country's largest union has afforded me countless opportunities, and I have met an incredible array of leaders and activists throughout the globe. None has inspired me to the degree that Jack did. He was my leader and my friend. The "project" will indeed continue.

Becoming Grandpa Jack
SARAH LAYTON

It was election night in the fall of 2008, and the Guvernment Bar in downtown Toronto was full of energy. After being asked to do a quick interview with my brother for a national news broadcaster, I was glad to escape to a room in the back that had been set up for my father and other family members so we could watch as the results came in later that night. I was about eight weeks pregnant, tired, nauseated, but so excited. My husband Hugh and I had been revealing our news to all sides of our family as we saw them over the course of that Thanksgiving weekend. My dad and Olivia were the last ones to tell.

My father had never pressured me to start having children but he always glowed when he talked about how much he enjoyed spending time with his own grandparents, one of whom the family called Grandpa Jack. One summer after a trip to British Columbia, he mentioned how it would be a great place to get away with grandkids one day. After that, he was careful to only drop subtle hints that maybe he was ready to play the role of Grandpa himself.

Eventually he and Olivia joined us and a few others in that back room to watch the results come in on two televisions set to different news channels. He asked how Hugh and I were doing and if we had recovered from making the big turkey lunch for the entire NDP campaign tour bus a few days earlier. We all settled in for a long evening. There is always a sense of nervousness and excitement on election night, and this one was no exception, but my head was elsewhere. I'm sure I didn't look as excited as I might have when we realized that the NDP had picked up some new seats. I just sipped on my ginger ale and tried to stay awake.

After joining the crowds in the packed main room to watch my dad and Olivia's victory speeches, I knew the time was almost right. He had finished several media interviews, made a few phone calls, shared big hugs with the team, and had a beer. We decided to walk with him, Olivia, and the RCMP team that follows him during elections to the car that was waiting for them. Finally, the perfect moment. As we all gave each other hugs goodnight, I looked my dad straight in the eye and said "Congratulations, Grandpa

Jack." He paused, looked at Olivia, then looked back at me. A huge smile came over his face and his eyes got glassy as he leaned in for another hug.

When they finally made it out of the building, I hear that he cried tears of joy the whole way home. He was ready to take on one of his proudest roles, that of Grandpa Jack.

Building Bridges to the Caucus
DI McINTYRE

Jack seldom had meetings at my house where he was staying, but one evening he had a tight schedule and what turned out to be overlapping engagements. A reporter had arrived (unexpected by me) for a scheduled interview just as I was serving homemade soup to two hungry MPs in my kitchen. The juggling was complicated by the fact that Jack hadn't arrived yet.

I had the reporter wait in the living room while Libby Davies and Svend Robinson talked quietly in the kitchen. After Jack had arrived and the interview was completed, I left these three friends to have a lively discussion. Libby and Svend had been the only caucus members to openly support Jack's leadership bid. They had both known him as a city councillor and through his work with the Federation of Canadian Municipalities. These two friends were a great support as Jack built bridges to the rest of the caucus.

Jack came home late one night in very good cheer—and filled with very good cheer. He had spent the evening in Bill Blaikie's office—the two were getting to know each other better while downing the better part of a bottle of good scotch that Jack had purchased. Another evening I invited

the whole caucus for a barbecue at One Renfrew Avenue—
the NDP had only fourteen MPs then. It was a comfortable,
warm summer night, and our garden provided an informal,
homey setting where everyone could mingle, away from
the pressures of the Hill. I bought a huge orange ice bucket
and filled it with everyone's favourite libations. Jack was, as
always, fun to be with and I could feel that the whole team
was coming to enjoy working with him. (I was introduced to
most of them affectionately as "Cousin Di," and that's the
way they referred to me: I'm sure that many still don't know
my last name!)

Gathering the Wisdom
BRAD LAVIGNE

Other than his family, the most important people to Jack
were his caucus. "Without them, we have nothing," he
would say. He told caucus members that he viewed his
week through the lens not of Monday to Sunday but of
Wednesday to Wednesday, the day caucus would meet. Jack
described these confidential weekly sessions as "gathering
the wisdom" because they were an opportunity to hear what
was on the minds of caucus and, more importantly, their
constituents. Indeed, the MPs with their fingers on the pulse
of their ridings reported each week with uncanny accuracy.

His approach to caucus came from his dad, Bob Layton,
who served as Brian Mulroney's caucus chair from 1986 to
1993. Bob Layton passed away just eight months before Jack
was elected NDP leader, and his picture hung directly over
Jack's desk in his Parliament Hill office as a source of daily
inspiration.

Every Wednesday morning, Jack's chief of staff, Anne McGrath, and I would meet with Jack for one final review of that morning's caucus meeting agenda and his report, which kicked off each meeting and set the tone. There was very little improvisation. The report would provide a recap of the previous week and the strategic direction for the upcoming week. Jack answered the question, "What's the game plan this week?"

But it wasn't the report itself that was the most important thing for Jack. He had learned from his dad and through conversations with former Prime Minister Mulroney that caucus solidarity and loyalty is not something that is just granted—rather it is earned and needs to be worked at each and every day.

Following Jack's report, there would be the all-important roundtable of the entire caucus, a format that began when the caucus was much smaller and each MP could weigh in on pretty much every issue without any time constraints. As the caucus grew, pressure mounted to drop the round-tables. Jack insisted that they stay—and they did. Jack would listen intently to each MP's intervention and be sure to take notes. He would even assign work to senior staff from his BlackBerry to handle the problem the MP was identifying while they were still talking.

Following the roundtable came the most important aspect for Jack: his wrap-up and closing remarks. It was here that caucus members would be looking for whether their problem had been heard. There was no script, no teleprompter, no meeting with colleagues or his staff to craft the response. It was just Jack, and it was one of the many areas in which he excelled. As a musician and as a politician, he was pitch perfect more often than not. He knew exactly what to say and the tone it needed to be delivered in.

At one meeting in the leadup to the 2008 election, an MP started fretting about the rise in popularity of a smaller party at our expense and pleaded with Jack to retool the entire strategy to reverse this "cataclysmic" turn of events. Those who followed began to become infected with the same fear and many MPs were in a full lather by the end of the roundtable. Jack listened intently, nodding in an understanding manner. When they were done, it was his turn. He put down his pen, cleared his throat, and said, "My old swim coach used to tell me, 'Don't worry about the swimmer that's behind you: concern yourself with the swimmer in front of you. He's the one you want to pass.' I listened to that strategy and won more races than if I hadn't. And we're going to do the same in the next campaign."

And with that came a collective sigh of relief and an understanding that their leader knew how to listen and focus. He never dismissed an MP or their concerns no matter how trivial they may have appeared. He knew the strength that was around that table. He knew that everyone had something to contribute and it was his job as leader to draw it out. That's why his caucus was unwaveringly loyal to him and followed him in bloody battles each and every day.

Love in Politics
BILL FREEMAN

Jack was engaged with his life and the people around him. Nothing reflects that engagement as much as his love of Olivia. It was a marvel to behold. Once, during Jack's first term as leader of the NDP in Ottawa, I was invited to a formal Ottawa dinner honouring writers. Jack was at the banquet, squeezed off at one of the back tables. He was, after all, then the leader of the fourth political party in the House of Commons. Naturally, he was surprised to find me there, and we chatted for a bit. At the end I said, "Jack, if there is anything I can do, just ask."

He locked my eyes with his and gripped my hand: "Get Olivia elected!"

I had my marching orders, and I don't doubt that hundreds of others had been told the same thing: "Get Olivia elected!" Jack needed her in Ottawa and it was up to us to deliver her. And we did.

Jack and Olivia celebrated the twentieth anniversary of their wedding at Paulette's and my house on Seneca Avenue on Algonquin Island. They wanted to be on the island because they were married at the Algonquin Island Association, but also because they felt close to Toronto Island residents and liked to share in our way of life. At times they said they wanted to be Islanders, but I expect this was more of a dream than a possibility. They were far too busy to live life according to the ferry schedule. Maybe they felt more like honourary Islanders because we had included them in so many things, from Caribana to Island dances. In any case, they wanted to celebrate their anniversary here and Islanders were only too happy to help make it happen.

The night of the event, Jack and Olivia pitched in with the preparations. The house was packed with people, and I know that Jack talked to everyone there. In the middle of the party, before the cake was cut, Jack gave a political speech—he never missed an opportunity to convert political disbelievers. It was a wonderful event enlivened by the infectious optimism and the good cheer of both Jack and Olivia.

I know you are not going to believe this but it's true: at the end of the evening, after everyone had gone home, there were about three cases of beer and some wine left over. Jack and Olivia were having a party in the city a couple of nights later and they needed that beer and wine. My last vision of Jack that night was of him handing Ralph, who runs the water taxi, the cases of beer. It was pitch black, and I was afraid he was going to step off the end of the dock into the water; but there he was, the leader of the federal New Democratic Party, hauling cases of beer because there were more events to host, more votes to win, and more people to convince of the importance of the NDP cause. Now that's a leader.

Music
SARAH LAYTON

My father was one of those people who could pick up a guitar or sit at a piano and just play. He had perfect pitch, could pick up any tune, keep the beat, and just seemed to be in his element.

He came from a music-loving family. In the weeks before he passed away, we spoke about family gatherings during his childhood, and how they all involved music. When he reminisced about Christmas traditions, he took an emotional pause as he remembered singing beside his father on many Christmas Eves. Bob Layton had a magnificent voice and was not afraid to use it. Dad missed that strong voice leading the songs with such passion.

Growing up, I remember him playing a number of instruments—guitar, piano, harmonica, his Layton Brothers organ, and even saxophone for a short while. Almost every time he travelled, he packed either a compact acoustic guitar or a fold-up electric piano.

I also remember the glass panes in our living room doors shaking with Pink Floyd's "Another Brick in the Wall" blasting through the house as he worked on his thesis. Then there was the whistling while we walked down the street. He was a fantastic whistler, but it was always met with an eye roll from me or a request to stop from my brother. But I admit that this came in handy because he had a special tune he would whistle when we were kids so that we could find him in a crowd.

When the Blue Jays won the World Series, he couldn't help running with his newly-acquired saxophone over to where the crowds had gathered on Yonge Street to blast out, "We are the Champions." When I was a teenager, he came to volunteer at the small summer camp I worked at and shared songs with the campers around the campfire. He raised funds for the Stephen Lewis Foundation once by singing and playing guitar on the side of the main street in his riding.

For anyone who has ever been to Jack and Olivia's house, or been camping with them, or on an election trail, or just about any situation in between, you might know how excited he became when someone, normally him, broke out a guitar. He would pass songbooks around and encourage everyone to join in. Can't sing? Here's a tambourine! I wonder how many people learned to sing "Barrett's Privateers" with him on guitar or "Hit the Road, Jack" with him on piano.

It wasn't just singing and playing music that interested him. That man could dance! He danced in the street at Caribana and at Pride Parades and generally was never afraid to get into the music. I remember him dancing and playing air guitar at my wedding. Thankfully my friends were kind enough not to post photos of this hilarious act on the Internet, although my father wouldn't have minded at all.

So after a lifetime of helping to entertain us and get us singing along, the family spent the final hours of his life singing to him. We couldn't find any of his favourite song-books—he always ordered them in bulk and then always gave them all away—but we sang anyway.

When my father's remains were leaving the Parliament buildings in August after lying in state, the bells chimed the "Dominion March," a piece of music written by his great-grandfather. He used to play it on the family organ which sat in his living room and would tell the tales of his family's rich musical roots. As I stood with our family there on the steps, we had a little chuckle. We never realized how long the song was because we had never let him play it in its entirety. There was always another good song to get to.

"I Like That Man!"
DI McINTYRE

Children saw the goodness and sincerity at the core of Jack, and he in turn loved children. He planned to be here in Ottawa for Hallowe'en 2004 to greet neighbourhood chil-dren at the door. He had asked me to buy treats to hand out, but wanted me to be sure that they were "Canadian-made, organic, and sugarless." So we had bowls full of locally-made organic fruit bars for children and parents. Jack delighted in talking to the children and asking about their costumes. Many of them remember him affectionately.

By chance, I met some neighbours at the Parliament

Hill candlelight vigil for Jack. Simon French, age five, had insisted that his family be there to say goodbye to Jack, even though it was hours past his bedtime. The previous April, Simon had watched the last leadership debate with his dad and had asked, "Who is that man?" When he was told that it was Jack Layton, he said, "I like that man!"

He woke his dad early on the morning of May 3 to ask if Jack had won. Simon, like so many of us, teared up when he heard that Jack had not become our prime minister.

Being Serious without Being Solemn
SUSAN BAKER

Jack was my city councillor and then my member of Parliament, and I worked on several of his campaigns; but my closest connection to Jack was through our mutual passion for the nonprofit organization I run, the Riverdale Share Community Association. Over the past twenty years, our organization has grown from a gaggle of neighbours mounting a community Christmas concert to a registered nonprofit with hundreds of volunteers raising hundreds of thousands of dollars for local organizations that support families in crisis in our community.

Jack found us in the early years, even before he was our city councillor. He loved music, he loved grassroots community involvement, and he truly believed that you could build a better Canada one person at a time, one community at a time. He made us believe it too. Jack jumped in with both feet, as Jack did with everything. He introduced us to potential sponsors, wrote letters of support, and assisted us in the registration process, but his biggest contribution was his time. In nineteen years Jack missed only one show. After he became leader of the NDP and was spending much of his time in Ottawa or traversing the country, I would receive text messages of his whereabouts as he rushed from the airport to get to the show on time. Once there he did whatever we needed done: handing out programs, on-stage pitches for donations, singing, playing guitar, dancing, auctioneering, and even donning the Santa suit when our regular Santa was sick.

I remember receiving word that our regular Santa had come down with the flu the day before our December 2003 concert. We absolutely could not have a show without the traditional arrival of Santa and, this close to Christmas, there were no Santas to be found. I believe it was Richard Barry, who sat on our volunteer committee at the time, who suggested that Jack play Santa. This was a busy time in Jack's life (as if there was a time in Jack's life that wasn't busy). He had recently been elected party leader and was revving up to run federally in our riding. I thought playing Santa would fall pretty far down his priority list, but I was wrong. A few quick emails later, we had our new Santa! Even though there was no mention of who was actually inside the Santa suit, Jack's voice and enthusiasm were pretty recognizable. He was the best, and the slimmest, Santa we ever had.

If Jack hadn't become a politician, I can imagine him as a performer. You could put him on a stage anywhere, any time, and he would capture the attention of the audience. In 1997, Jack was onstage at the Danforth Music Hall doing his usual pitch for donations when we sent a message out with my five-year-old daughter Olivia, who was dressed as a sugar plum fairy. Jack took the piece of paper, but then unexpectedly engaged her in conversation. He told her that "Olivia" was his favourite name in the whole world as it was the name of his true love. She smiled ear-to-ear and then told him that "Jack" was her favourite name. He asked why that was and she responded that "Jack" was the name of her dog. The little skit was completely impromptu but they replayed it over for years whenever they ran into each other. After that, people often asked me if I had actually named my daughter Olivia and my dog Jack after Olivia Chow and Jack Layton. Just for the record I would like to say that I did not, but it turned out to be a happy coincidence.

The following year, we asked all our Toronto–Danforth elected officials to participate in the show by performing as a Christmas Country Bluegrass Band. Paula Fletcher, a gifted singer, was our school trustee; Jack, an accomplished musician, was our city councillor; Marilyn Churley was our MPP; and Dennis Mills, the only Liberal in the group, was our MP. Marilyn's then-boyfriend/now-husband Richard Barry and a couple of our professional band members rounded out the act.

They all dressed in jeans and plaid shirts and we gave them instruments such as spoons and washboards and basins, but Jack played the guitar. Even after a few rehearsals the painfully long act didn't go smoothly; everyone was off time and off key. But near the end, Jack leaned into the mike and made the observation that even though he, Marilyn, and Paula were all standing stage left and Dennis was standing stage right, they could still make beautiful music together. Since his passing, I have heard many people talk about Jack's admirable ability to work with everyone regardless of whether they shared his views.

Jack had an amazing talent for auctioneering, and we weren't the only organization to take full advantage of it. At our annual spring fundraiser, "Bebop-a-looza," the live auction by Jack was a much-anticipated part of the event. He had the ability to auction off anything and everything, and he did. If it wasn't nailed down you'd see Jack hauling it up onto the stage—including two sets of $9.99 plastic patio lanterns I had brought from home to decorate the silent-auction table, for which Jack managed to get $200 per set.

One of the most touching and memorable auction moments took place in 2009. The It's My Party store on the Danforth had donated a huge stuffed horse. Jack got the auction rolling and the first bid of five dollars was made by seven-year-old Jordan Decker. Jordan had $20 saved from her allowance, but the bidding was escalating rapidly and Jordan was soon out of the running. Jack kept bringing it back to Jordan, who stood right in front of the stage long-ingly admiring the horse. I was confused as to why he kept doing this, as it was pretty obvious that Jordan would not have the ability to compete. The horse sold for $200, but when Jack asked the successful bidder to come up and claim his horse, the bidder announced that he would like to give the horse to the little girl with the opening bid. All eyes were on Jordan as she squealed in excitement, ran up to the stage, and wrapped her arms around the horse, which stood taller than she did. She said, "Thank you, Jack Layton," and he said, "Thank you for being so cute." I caught Jack's eye and he winked at me. This had been his plan all along.

After the Riverdale Share concert we always held a big party back at my house for the volunteers and performers to celebrate yet another successful year. Jack rarely missed one. Often he would disappear upstairs to my office to do a tele-phone interview or participate in a conference call before he would wade into the crowd and be drawn into one conversation after another.

Over the years he had developed quite a close relationship with my cleaning lady, Lolita. She knew that by the time Jack made it to the buffet table, his favourite honey-basted ham would surely have been devoured. So every year Lolita would make up a plate for Jack and keep it warm in the oven to ensure that he had a nice hot dinner. (I somehow imagine Olivia's mother, Mrs. Chow, doing the same thing.) Lolita and Jack always had their little chat and he always asked about her family. When I received an invitation, for myself and a guest, to attend the Celebration of Jack's Life, I took Lolita. He would have liked that.

Pubs
DI McINTYRE

Jack enjoyed going out to unwind and listen to music. One of his favourite haunts was the Rainbow in Ottawa's market area. One night we coaxed MP Jean Crowder from B.C. to join us there after an evening reception on the Hill and we all danced until the wee hours.

Sometimes Jack would call late in the evening and ask if I'd had dinner. Whether I had or not, it was a chance to talk with Jack, so I'd walk to meet him. We often chose the Clock Tower Brew Pub in the Glebe, where the kitchen is open until midnight and where the salads served with blackened salmon or steak are always a treat. We'd sit at one of the high tables by the bar. Often, even in his early days in Ottawa, Jack was recognized, and people would approach to chat. Jack was always receptive and open, respectfully listening and engaging in easy exchanges.

Romancing Quebec—1
REBECCA BLAIKIE

Just before the 2004 election, Jack called me at my apartment in Montreal to persuade me to run as a candidate in Quebec. The tone of his voice was optimistic. He told me we were building and that this election was another important step towards a breakthrough for our movement in La Belle Province. The thought of running had not crossed my mind, but Jack presented it as an exciting opportunity to contribute. The NDP was nearly nonexistent in Quebec, such that even a small campaign would be beneficial to our political presence. When I called my father to discuss the possibility, he suggested that if I was going to run, I "might as well go after the big guy." His suggestion made sense to me, and Jack loved the idea. Shortly thereafter I became the federal NDP candidate in LaSalle-Émard, running against Prime Minister Paul Martin. Even over the phone, Jack had a way of making you feel indispensable to the movement. It turned out to be the start of a great partnership.

What I learned as a candidate in Quebec was quite simply that although the vast majority of the folks I met on the campaign trail shared the values and vision of the NDP, very few Québécois knew the NDP existed. They had started to hear about Jack and were warming to his personality but there was much work to be done. Inspired by my experience, I continued to work with the federal party and became director of organization for the 2006 federal election campaign in Quebec. For the next three years we journeyed together, bringing the message of *l'NPD* to the *peuple Québécois*. Getting to know Jack was one of the great perks of the job.

One of my favourite moments with Jack was a trip we

took in 2007 to celebrate *La Saint-Jean* in Quebec City. Jack had already made a habit of celebrating the *fête nationale* by attending the grand parade in Montreal, and he was always well received. At that time, no other federal leaders were willing to take the risk of celebrating this important day.

In 2007 we were in full breakthrough strategy mode, and Jack had decided to spend two full days in Quebec to highlight the national holiday. Staffing the leader in this kind of situation—at his best, among the people in a festive environment—was a privilege and a pleasure. It offered an opportunity to spend quality time with Jack. And Jack excelled in these circumstances. He was able to run from one thing to the next. He could make the very most of every hour and somehow manage to remain engaging and interested in all the people he met along the way.

Typically on such a day—and this was no exception—Jack would go straight from the airport to a *cinq à sept*. Usually these were attended by a combination of party faithful (yes, there were some even then!), young and soft sovereignists looking for a new home, disaffected Liberals looking for inspiration, and straight-up fans of the charismatic "M. Clayton." He made all of them feel important, and he genuinely believed they were.

Once sufficient *cinq à sept* schmoozing was done, we moved on to mainstreeting down the Grande-Allée. Jack was stunned by his own popularity that day, as were we. It seemed everyone we passed recognized him and wanted their picture taken with him, to shake his hand, or just thank him for being there. This was one those moments where the breakthrough we were working towards became tangible, and that gave us the energy we needed to keep working at it. Our next stop was a fancier event and, after a quick change of clothes in the car, he was working another crowd.

As we left the cocktail event, a sudden storm drenched us on the way to the car. Nicolas-Dominic Audet picked us up, and it was clear we had to take Jack somewhere to dry off. Nico decided to surprise his friends, a Tunisian couple new to Quebec City who lived nearby. They had never met Jack and could not yet vote, but within moments Jack had accepted their invitation for coffee and was deep in conversation with our gracious hosts. So deep, in fact, that we had trouble extricating him from it: it took great persistence. One of Jack's strengths was that he wasn't just good in a crowd—he was also good with individuals. In conversation, he listened sincerely to people's stories. The pace he kept may sometimes have been frustrating for him in that regard: he was constantly meeting people and starting great conversations, only to be cut off by a staffer and chivvied along to the next person or meeting or event.

Once our clothes were dry, we moved on. Jack was to attend a gala event without us, so in the car came the briefing: who was who, whom to be sure you speak to, these are the issues they may raise, etc. But for all the politics, it was really personality that Jack had going for him in Quebec at that time.

For those of us who had the privilege of working closely with Jack on the "Quebec project," these moments with him were inspiring and motivating. In these instances we were able to see the draw and strength of our leader, and the incredible potential he brought to our movement.

It was a day that ended emotionally around a table in Quebec's Vieux Port, meeting with one of the candidates who would eventually be part of the 2011 orange wave. Over dinner that evening we saw another side of Jack. We were moved by the sincere sadness and rage he felt at the injustices, past and present, faced by Aboriginal people in Canada. Jack went on to work relentlessly to force the official residential schools apology. It was an apology that he hoped would be the start of a new relationship built on respect. In his vision the apology was only the first step on a healing journey of meaningful reconciliation and justice over many years.

Our evening ended on the highway to Montreal, the leader sleeping in the back seat. It was important he be ready for the grand parade in the morning. We knew he would be well received and welcomed with open arms by the thousands of Québécois who would be waiting on Sherbrooke Street. It was through these moments of sincerity and connection that Jack came to truly understand, and thus receive, the affection of a nation.

Romancing Quebec—2
NICOLAS-DOMINIC AUDET

I went to Ottawa during the first weeks of the new session in 2011. Having run Romeo Saganash's campaign, I had been away from my usual action for the duration of the campaign period. (I had been in the central office during the 2006 and 2008 elections.)

Heading north with my friend Romeo was both a challenge and an honour, but it was the first time that I had given myself 100 per cent to a single campaign. So I was far from both my usual gang and my regular election beat. Fortunately, the boss's tour included a visit to us in Val d'Or. Our riding was a high priority.

That gave me one more opportunity to brief Jack—who knew it would be my last?

As usual, Jack listened carefully and asked the usual questions for about fifteen minutes. I found him hugely energetic despite his weight loss during the previous weeks. He did what I had seen him do many times before: he made a terrific speech to a crowd that expected nothing less. What was new was such a good turnout in a town like Val d'Or—a clue to what was going to happen on May 2.

Then, at the end of May, I came back to Parliament Hill for an amazing event: the group photo of all 103 NDP MPs. In that room, I reconnected with many friends and activists I had met over the last six years and, at the end of the day, I was able to meet up with my communications buddies. As I walked down the street, I came across Jack, followed by his closest advisors.

Jack really knew how to handle his people and give us personal recognition. He thanked me for all my work over the years and said that I had played a very important role in our party's success. Then he hugged me. It would be the last time I saw him.

A Change of Heart
WILLY BLOMME

The first time I met Jack I was not impressed. Growing up in a progressive Toronto family, I had always known who he was and admired the work that he and Olivia did at City Hall; but when I met him for the first time in April of my second year at McGill I was put off. Rumours of an NDP leadership race were rampant and Jack's name was already being bandied about as a likely contender. He was scheduled to give a talk to the McGill NDP about homelessness; as I was the co-chair of the New Democratic Youth of Canada (NDYC) at the time, Svend Robinson and Jack's nephew had arranged for him to meet with me beforehand at Gert's, the campus bar. To my surprise I found him overbearing and phony. For the hour or so that we sat at the bar he spoke incessantly about various projects he had spearheaded. I left the bar disappointed and put the encounter out of mind to study for my finals.

A few months later I found myself sharing a billet with Jack in Calgary during the G20 protests. Every hotel room in town had been booked, so his staff had called me to ask if I could help find him a place to stay, as I was one of the organizers of the NDYC workshops at the protest. I didn't have much time, so I simply asked my own billet, my university roommate's family. Because we were staying at the same house, Jack and I spent a lot of time together during the protest: at the workshops organized by the NDYC, where he gave his presentation sitting cross-legged on the grass in a circle of two dozen young activists; at the big march, where people from across the country streamed up to him to shake his hand or thank him for the help he had given to their local projects; and at a dinner with a local developer turned homelessness activist.

At the end of a long day packed full of events, Jack and I sat for the first time with time to kill while we waited for the C-Train to take us home. That's when I got to know the real Jack. He started asking me about my experience at McGill. He asked about papers I had written and classes that inspired me. Then he wanted to know what had made me get involved in politics and my vision for Canada. He asked about how I thought we could push the country in the right direction. As the conversation progressed I found myself talking more and more. And Jack continued to prod. I realized he wasn't just making polite conversation. He was genuinely interested in what I had to say. Even though he had been involved in politics longer than I had been alive, he treated me as a peer. He wanted to hear my ideas and brainstorm about how to achieve them. That was when I realized that the Jack I had met at Gert's was not an act. He had not been showing off and trying to impress a potential campaign supporter. He was truly inspired by the potential of the projects he was involved with and wanted to bring others on board. I understood that Jack was a man of boundless energy and a determination to make the country a better place.

Working on his leadership campaign, we all got to know—and sometimes curse—Jack's energy and ideas. Sitting in a staff meeting several months into the campaign, the campaign manager, Bruce Cox, suddenly exclaimed, "Oh God, Jack is off the plane!" Jack had spent the hour in the air between events translating his new ideas into emails on his BlackBerry. The minute the plane touched down he hit "send," bombarding Bruce's inbox with a slew of new emails. Weeks later Bruce accompanied Jack on a weekend trip to southern Ontario where three debates were being held in two days. At the end of the weekend Bruce was driving him home, exhausted. As they neared his home, Jack said, "Could you drop me off at the corner here? There is a Chinese Garment Workers Association meeting happening and I want to pop in to say hello."

It was in Calgary that I discovered another one of Jack's great talents. The morning after our C-Train station chat Jack had to catch an early flight. My roommate's father, a prominent Calgary Liberal, offered to drive him out to the airport but made the mistake of driving one of the family's two SUVs. For the duration of the trip, Jack prattled on informatively about the evils of SUVs. Amazingly, John returned home amused rather than annoyed. Jack did not convince John to switch parties, but I did hear a rumour that John had donated to Jack's leadership campaign. It was not a fully successful recruitment, but the first step to building common ground as only Jack could.

The Chair
BRIAN TOPP

At the end of the May 2011 campaign Jack Layton was on his way to the peak of his career. A hundred and three seats! Official Opposition status! A leap over the Liberals and the Bloc! He was also exhausted, beginning to worry about his health again, and still limping as a result of his recent hip surgery.

Election day was eerily quiet for the candidate and his team. The events were over; all across the country the party was busy getting out the vote; and so there were long hours to wait. Jack spent most of his time on election day in his hotel suite, calling candidates, thinking about what might come next, and talking to his family, his staff, and his campaign team.

Finally, mid-evening, the results. The results! And then a long, relatively slow walk down long corridors, down elevators, and along more long corridors to the hall where Jack would greet a new political era.

We showed up too early and ended up in a homely service corridor—some family, some staff, a television crew doing a colour documentary on Layton's election day, and Jack. He was visibly hurting from the long walk and uncomfortable standing for the fifteen minutes or so we needed to wait.

So we got him a chair. Which he refused to sit in. "I can't sit in a chair if everyone else has to stand," he said.

It was another moment to remember Jack's strongly held principles. He rejected entitlements. And he cared about other people. Even when we really needed him to sit down in that chair, so that he'd be okay to stand in front of his party and the country and greet the results.

What to do?

I said, "Well, I'm going to sit down." And I sat on the floor, next to the chair. Jack laughed: "Okay, now we're equal." And he took the chair.

It made for a weird image when broadcast the following day: Jack on his chair, me on the floor, and the rest of the team standing around us. It was also the essence of the man—generous, egalitarian, communitarian. And determined to live those principles as well as he could.

Jack and Olivia riding in the Pride Parade in Toronto, 2005.

Jack speaks to an audience in 2005, two years after becoming leader of the NDP.

Jack and Luba Goy on the set of Air Farce in 2006.

Courtesy of Luba Goy

Jack participating in a singalong before the 2007 Riverdale Share Christmas show.

Courtesy of Susan Baker

Jack and Olivia rafting on the Alsek River, Kluane, Alaska, 2008.
Courtesy of Bruce Kirby

Jack, looking relaxed and fit, in 2008.
Courtesy of New Democratic Party of Canada

Jack and Richard Barry busking on the Danforth in Toronto in 2009 to raise money for the Stephen Lewis Foundation.

Courtesy of Marilyn Churley

Jack auctioning off a toy horse at Bebop-a-looza 2010.

Courtesy of Susan Baker

Jack campaigning, just before the 2011 federal election.
Courtesy of New Democratic Party of Canada

Jack celebrating the NDP's new status as Official Opposition in June 2011.
Courtesy of New Democratic Party of Canada

Olivia looking at mementoes left at a makeshift memorial to Jack on Parliament Hill on August 25, 2011.

CP Images

5

Jack's Legacy

Jack gave us many gifts, but the greatest may be the ways he showed that politics could be done differently.

At a time when political obfuscation and outright lying reigned, when personal attacks and misrepresentations were commonplace, when withholding information and resources was acceptable, and when widening the holes in the social safety net was just the way it had to be, Jack reminded us that there are other possibilities.

He showed us by example that one could debate the issues rather than merely attack people; that politics could be inclusive rather than exclusionary; that all voices could be heard, not silenced; and that all people, not just voters and taxpayers, matter.

He was proof that a decent man could live his principles in love, in friendship, and in government.

We need more Jacks in this country. We need more Jacks in the world.

A Gentle Hug
MARILYN CHURLEY

I knew Jack was in an uphill battle with cancer, but I also knew that if anyone could beat it, Jack could. He was an incredible optimist and never wavered in his belief that he was going to get better. As my husband Richard, who worked with him for many years, said, "You just don't go to Jack with a problem unless you have some solutions to offer." And mostly, whatever problem was presented to him, Jack working with others could find compromises, if not solutions. I am sure Jack continued to expect the doctors and specialists to come up with the right solution until close to the very end.

I visited Jack about two weeks before he died. Before I walked into the room, I had braced myself for the worst. And it was bad. His daughter Sarah opened the door for me and I turned the corner to see Jack sitting in a recliner chair. He looked so very thin and fragile that I thought I might drop to the floor in anguish. But Jack saved me. His blue eyes looked huge in his thin face and they lit up like stars when he saw me. He gave me the most joyous smile, and even though his voice was weak, it was enthusiastic and spirited as he said, "Marilyn, I am so glad to see you." It was as if his indelible spirit leapt out at me and for a while it was like old times. Except of course it wasn't.

We never talked directly of his impending death. We spoke of our families (we both spoke proudly of our grandchildren) and he wanted to hear all about my road trip back home to Labrador with my two sisters. We talked of our friendship and all the things we had worked on together and all the fun we had had. We spoke of his legacy and what he had accomplished. We spoke of spirituality and his deep belief that there was an afterlife of some sort, but he didn't know what it was. And he told me repeatedly how much the cards and emails and gifts helped sustain him through the last hard few months. It was abundantly clear that at the end Jack felt appreciated and sheltered in the love and good wishes coming from all over the country every day. It really did mean so very much to him.

When it was time to go, I briefly left the room to pull myself together so I could be strong as we said goodbye. I wasn't sure if I could do it. But when I re-entered the room, there was Jack, giggling as he struggled to stand up in the middle of the floor, leaning on Sarah and an aide. He said, "Come here." I walked towards him and asked if we could hug. He said, "Yes, but gently." We carefully put our arms around each other and then looked deeply into each other's eyes. Not a word said, but gentle smiles. We both knew this was our last goodbye and we said it between the lines.

Before Richard and I left for our vacation at our cottage I left a soft, plush, orange blanket on his doorstep. Olivia emailed me to tell me that Jack said it was a perfect gift, that it was soft and cuddly and that he had it beside him in bed. We had been at the cottage only two days when I received a text from Olivia early in the morning telling me that Jack had passed on and that he had died with my orange blanket beside him. We drove back to Toronto to be with Jack's other close friends.

I was lucky to be asked to act as one of Jack's honourary pallbearers—a state funeral no less! It was such a great and powerful send-off for Jack, and he would have loved every minute of it!

I miss my friend Jack. But I know his spirit is strong and abiding and will live on with us forever.

The Last Day
DI McINTYRE

Jack's final arrival on Parliament Hill on August 24, 2011, was a day filled with sadness.

The family were asked to be at the Hill early. Jack's staff had arranged for me to have a parking spot next to the Centre Block and I had a wheelchair for Mom. It was a very moving sign with hundreds of people lined up to sign the book of condolences. Four of us checked through security and then were escorted to the main hall of the Centre Block, where we waited beside a red carpet. After what seemed a very long wait, the NDP caucus members arrived and stood sombrely across the red carpet from us. A few nodded to me, and Jack Harris crossed the carpet to bring Mom a handkerchief and say a few words. We had lost someone who had a big place in our hearts, someone who had inspired and encouraged us. We had lost him so quickly. There was no protocol for this.

We heard the skirl of bagpipes and watched as the casket was slowly, steadily walked up the front stairs by RCMP officers, followed by Olivia, Sarah and Hugh Campbell with their daughter Beatrice, Michael with fiancée Brett Tryon, Sally, and Hedley Roy. We wheeled in behind and gathered in the Opposition Lobby while the casket was set on a stand. It gave us a few minutes to talk with Olivia and the family. Then we each had a chance to view the casket and say our goodbyes. I realized too late that this was our chance to sign the book, to be the first in the book, but none of us did.

Sadly, Jack is no longer sitting in Parliament representing Canadians, but he left us with powerful messages that we can make the world a better place if we love one another and remain hopeful and optimistic. All of us, young and old, have valuable contributions to make to our communities. Let's not miss the chance to serve. Change is possible, if we work fearlessly together.

Since his passing dozens of people have written or called to share with me the memorable conversations and special moments they had with Jack at my house, at events, or in airports. There is a common thread to these stories, often about the first time that they had an opportunity to talk to him personally. Jack always had time to say hello. Once he'd met someone, he never forgot them; whatever the length of time between meetings he would remember not only their names but also what they had talked about. Jack always left people feeling hopeful and excited about the future.

Deep-fried Pepperoni
KARL BÉLANGER

It was a cold February evening in Sydney, Cape Breton. Jack Layton and I had had a long day of doing what one does in politics, outside the parliamentary arena.

We had started the day in Halifax, first joined by MP Peter Stoffer for a meeting with Rear Admiral Bob Davidson. Then Layton spoke at a conference of the Nova Scotia Young New Democrats, followed by a lunch with the delegates. After that we flew to Sydney, where we had a meeting scheduled with a group of pensioners from Devco. The evening ended with the Leader's Levee in Cape Breton, a joint fundraiser with Nova Scotia NDP Leader Darrell Dexter at Sydney's Pensioners Club.

Long day then. When we were ready to wind down, he asked me to join him at the Crown and Moose pub located in the Delta Sydney where we were crashing for the night. We'll watch a game, he said: "And there is something I would like you to try."

Jack Layton enjoyed food. He was a fit man, exercising on a daily basis, and without keeping a strict diet he ate healthy food, most of the time. Avoiding bread and potatoes. Leaving sausages aside. "Nothing good can come from meat in a tube," he used to say. He'd go for healthy portions of vegetables. Salads. Fruits, granola, and yogurt for breakfast. But because he enjoyed food, he let himself indulge from time to time.

He had a couple of *péchés mignons* when it came to food. Beef—prime rib, especially. As I once said to Rick Mercer's camera, "He likes his meat." For sure, he did. When Layton first got to Ottawa he discovered the lamb shank at D'Arcy McGee's, which his D-Comm at the time described (wrongly) as "disgusting."

While travelling in the Prairies, for lunch or as a snack he regularly ordered dry ribs, a delicacy I discovered thanks to him. He liked a good slab of ribs too, and even asked an aide to fetch him an order from the International Chicken-Rib Cook-Off on Sparks Street as the debate about the back-to-work legislation was dragging on last June. He also loved his mother-in-law's Chinese New Year's feast—or anything she cooked, really.

What else? Well, peanut butter. "I could live off this stuff," he told me a few times. He was always surprised by the fact that I didn't drink coffee—he liked his black, no sugar. After the first cancer diagnosis, he switched to decaf, much to his dismay. In fact, his whole diet changed after the diagnosis—and Olivia made sure of it! Not that he was really undisciplined before: Jack always knew how many extra minutes of gym time he would need to burn off the extra calories he had consumed.

But back in 2004 in Sydney, none of these health concerns were on the radar screen as we sat down and ordered a pint. Jack didn't need to grab the menu. He'd been here before, during his travels as Federation of Canadian Municipalities president. So he simply asked for an order of pepperoni. What kind of finger food is that, I thought to myself?

But over the past few months, I had learned to trust Jack's capacity to order food in a restaurant. Seeing him in action in a Chinese restaurant was something else—he would order a few dishes for the table to share and do so in Cantonese, much to the pleasant surprise of the wait staff and other diners. And so once again, in Sydney's own British pub, I trusted him. Soon after, an order of Deep-fried Pepperoni arrived.

It was delicious. Salty. Greasy. Spicy. Hot. With honey mustard sauce on the side. It couldn't possibly be healthy. Never mind. It was a lot of fun.

So on the day Jack Layton passed away, as we were dealing with the shock and our sadness, lots of New Democrats and friends spontaneously assembled at Brixton's, our regular hangout on Sparks Street, to commiserate and share memories. Between interviews, I stopped by. I should eat something, I thought. I had been going nonstop since the morning.

I peered at the menu.

And I remembered.

Legend has it that Jack persuaded the staff at Brixton's to put it on the menu.

And to name it after him.

With a smile, I ordered *Jack's Deep-fried Pepperoni*.

A View from Down Under
TIM FLANNERY

"Hey, Jack Layton wants to meet you. How about that?"
Rob Firing, my publicist at HarperCollins, was consulting
his BlackBerry as we sat in a café, and was clearly impressed.
I, meanwhile, had just downed my third cup of coffee,
desperate to stay alert for the next interview, and the name
meant nothing to me. It was 2006 and I'd just published the
Canadian edition of *The Weather Makers*. With the book fast
climbing the bestseller lists, my tour was becoming a night-
mare of eighteen-hour days, and the jet lag after the flight
from Australia was relentless. Something about my body
language must have revealed that I was less than enthusiastic
about yet another meeting, but Rob was insistent. "I think
I can reschedule that interview on Tuesday so that you can
make lunch with Jack," he said as if it was already decided.

I was expecting to meet a politician of the type I was used
to in Australia—someone a little shifty, perhaps, who was
hoping to use me in some way. But the moment Jack walked
into the hotel lobby I knew he was different. It impressed
me that he had cycled to the meeting, and he talked not
about politics but about his commitment to the environment
and the work he had done with his father on clean-energy
projects. Jack also told me that he had given a copy of my
book to Stephen Harper, telling the prime minister that if
he did one thing during his holidays it should be to read it.
Of course I was flattered that Jack thought so highly of my
work and that he believed the book just might change the
way Canadians think about climate change.

As we parted that day Jack gave me a copy of his book
Speaking Out Louder. Unable to carry it about on tour, I

asked Rob if he could post it to me. Unfortunately, both of us were so frazzled that the book was forgotten. (It was only years later, when I emailed Rob letting him know that I'd be in Toronto for Jack's funeral, that his memory about the book was jogged. He said that he still had it in his office and would give it to me when we met up.)

Very soon Jack and I were to cross paths again, for Jack invited me to address the NDP federal convention in Quebec in September 2006. Of course I was delighted, and recall the honour of sharing the stage with Stephen Lewis and Malai Joya, a young female politician from Afghanistan who told the audience that Canada should withdraw its troops from her country, even if it meant that her own life would be endangered. But most of all it was the enthusiasm of the crowd that stayed with me. They were mad for Jack, and fired up about helping to create a better world.

After that, whenever I was in Canada, or Jack and I were attending an international meeting, we'd make sure to catch up. At COP15 in Copenhagen, in 2009, I had the privilege of introducing Jack and Olivia to Kevin Rudd, then the Australian prime minister. We all had high hopes for the outcome of that meeting, and initially the results disappointed us. But looking back I can see that it was a valuable stepping stone towards the Cancun and Durban meetings, at which the basis of negotiations for a legally binding global treaty (to be agreed to by 2015) was achieved. I just wish that Jack could have lived long enough to see that outcome, and to know that his efforts at Copenhagen contributed directly to the deal. I can imagine the smile that news would have brought to his face.

Whenever I visited Jack in Toronto he'd appear at the front door of his home wearing his "Aussie hat," as he called it. It was a broad-brimmed, battered-looking Akubra—the bushman's hat—and you could tell that Jack knew he was strikingly handsome in it. The dining room was invariably filled with family and friends discussing the issues of the day, from Afghanistan to climate change and bike lanes in Toronto. Jack's views were no different when he was nestled among his family than when he was in the public eye. He always spoke passionately, directly, and clearly. He was a person, and a politician, without guile.

Perhaps only a non-Canadian can appreciate how lucky Canada was to have Jack Layton. Everywhere the nature of politics is changing. Crass populism is on the rise, and with it the politics of greed, selfishness, and distrust. Jack was the antithesis of that. He cared passionately about the common good: gender equality, public transport, the environment, and Canada's leadership in the world. But he did not care about such things out of some arcane ideology or abstract idea. His starting point was love—a deep love of the people he met and led.

Politicians who care solely about power have the easiest job in the world. Just tell the people what they want to hear: The climate scientists are frauds, so there's no need to act on climate change; governments only waste money, so there's no need for taxation; and no point working together to achieve the common good. As the right-wing media spread fear, those arguments are winning everywhere. The great selfishness now sweeping the West is, I believe, just the first fruit of this politics of cynicism and greed. As it gains pace, our common wealth must dwindle, and the services provided by governments, as well as international co-operation, must begin to fail. Stare into the abyss that such a politics creates and you wonder where the bottom is: stripped of the trust that permits us to live together, the heart of humanity can be dark indeed.

For people the world over, Jack Layton was a bulwark against that descent into despair. He was the one who through his own boundless optimism and generosity of spirit coaxed us also to be generous, to trust, and to give of ourselves for the greater good. There is no politician like Jack Layton in Australia, the United States, or Europe. Sure, those places have left-leaning parties with great leaders. But no one I know can speak to the people about the things that matter the way Jack could. And so even non-Canadians who knew something of Canadian politics looked to Jack for inspiration.

Jack and I talked often of a visit to Australia. He had never been down under, and I'm sure he would have loved it. It would also have been good politics. Australia has now legislated its carbon tax and a raft of other measures to fight climate change, including a comprehensive package offering a $10 billion green-investment fund, tax cuts for the poorest, and protection for trade-exposed industry. It would be a great model for Canada to look to as it seeks to live up to its international obligations.

My visits to Canada often coincided with political events, and I was back for the 2011 federal election. As he hobbled from event to event nursing a broken hip, Jack seemed to lose whatever politician's gloss he had, and in its place there grew an intimacy with his audiences. It was as if we knew that he was speaking directly to you and me—to all of us, as individuals. And his message, regardless of the issue under discussion, was this: have faith in one another. Know that through the right sort of politics we can be kind, and responsible, and nurturing of one another—that together, we are unstoppable. For those few weeks of the campaign

Jack seemed unstoppable too. Had the campaign gone on much longer, it seemed possible that he might have been prime minister of Canada.

I was on a book tour as Jack was hobbling across the country. We planned to catch up, and I desperately wanted to see him—to shake his hand and say how much I admired him. But even more I wanted him to win. And I could see how tired he was. So we said that we'd catch up after the campaign, when he'd won. If I could have seen the future I would have made sure that we took the time to share a meal and talk before I returned to Australia. As it was, I finally caught up with him in August 2011, in a Roy Thomson Hall so full of love, goodwill, and determination to carry the flame that it seemed not that Jack was gone but that he was speaking from every Canadian heart.

I was back in Australia when I finally opened the book Jack had given me at our first meeting in 2006. As I read it while sitting in the sunlight on the verandah, discovering over again what a passionate and just man Jack Layton was, I found that he had left me one last message. On the fly-leaf of the book he'd written, "Dear Tim, with many thanks and a kindred spirit." I'd not cried at his funeral, but I wept quietly as I read those words, even though I knew that for people like Jack death is not the end of leadership, inspiration, or friendship.

A Gift of Hope
SUSAN BAKER

Jack was a walking symbol of hope. There was hope in his eyes and it exuded from every pore. As he went through life he happily gave chunks of that hope to those who crossed his path. To be touched by Jack was to be left hopeful and optimistic. When I read Jack's last message to Canadians, I realized that this was the gift he had given us all along: "My friends, love is better than anger. Hope is better than fear. Optimism is better than despair. So let us be loving, hopeful and optimistic. And we'll change the world."

When Jack stepped down to do battle with his last bout of cancer he said, "It is important to take time out, when life challenges us in other ways." In his last message he asked us "to cherish every moment with those you love at every stage of your journey." I took that advice to heart and decided to put the Riverdale Share Concert on hiatus for a year so that I would have the time to take care of my own father who is dying from cancer. His name, too, is Jack.

A Man with the Greatest of Hearts
MICHAEL KAUFMAN

Jack was a walking storybook. I don't mean he was one of those people always entertaining you with tales. I mean there was something about him that came right out of a storybook.

Sure, he could be a tough adversary, but he also had a boyish, Tom Sawyer–esque charm. I remember dropping in at his place one summer afternoon in the mid-1990s. It may have been to talk about the state of the White Ribbon Campaign, which we had co-founded in 1991, but I seem to recall it had something to do with the currently woeful state of my love life. Jack was out back. His job that day was cleaning out their fish pond: netting the goldfish and dropping them into a bucket, pumping the water out, and then climbing in and scraping out a couple of years' accumulation of fish droppings and decomposed plants that covered the bottom in a thick layer of repulsive, black mush.

Rather than "his job," I should have written "our job," for within minutes I too had my shoes and shirt off and was ankle and elbow deep in this disgusting mess. But here's the thing about Jack. Not only was it fun to do this together—as it's fun to do physical work with a friend with whom you spend much of the time talking—but Jack had a way of making you feel you were lucky to get to help out.

I had met Jack in the late 1980s through some local work in Toronto to raise awareness about men's violence against women, and again in 1989 when Gord Cleveland and I started a one-off national campaign called Men for Women's Choice. But it wasn't until 1991 that we really started to know each other. It was then, along with our colleague Ron Sluser and then men in several cities, that we started the White Ribbon Campaign. We took a novel approach in that the campaign was a decentralized effort that had no membership but saw itself as a catalyst to get good men out there raising their voices to end the violence being committed by some of our fathers, brothers, sons, neighbours, and friends.

Jack and I made a pretty good team, and there were some years when we were de facto half-time volunteers. We may have matched each other for big ideas, but he had a singular way of making them happen. He had a bit of Robin Hood about him: one day he announced he had arranged for a free office at the Eaton Centre; another he arrived with hand-me-down computers and a photocopier, when these were still very expensive items. He also had more than a touch of the Pied Piper going for him. He spoke and people wanted to follow. I don't mean speaking as an orator. Where he excelled was one-on-one, over a beer, standing face-to-face, or in a meeting. Even when he was on the public stage, he had a way of talking and acting exactly as he did in private: more than anyone else I've ever known, he moved gracefully, earnestly, and honestly between his public and private selves—in fact, such a distinction was hard to make.

One story speaks volumes about his commitment. It must have been 1994 or 1995. Jack and I, always the wild optimists, had persuaded our fellow members of the WRC board to mount big public campaigns between 1992 and 1994. We did huge mass mailings and hired occasional part-time staff. A truly massive debt piled up. Receiving no public funding, we relied on donations from individuals, companies, and unions, but it was clear this wasn't going to be enough to keep our heads above water. It looked like the end of the White Ribbon Campaign.

Jack came to me. He had arranged for a loan. The only hitch? To get this loan, Jack and Olivia had to use their house and I my car as collateral. This loan and years of hard work and fundraising by a dedicated group of volunteers got us over the hump and eventually allowed White Ribbon to develop into a professionally led organization. (The transformation was helped, actually, when Jack stepped away to run for the NDP leadership and when I did the same a few years later to focus on my writing and public-education work.)

It was one of those moments when dreams were crunching against a harsh financial reality, when powers of persuasion seemed to trip over themselves. In effect, Jack said we needed to take a personal risk, to tip the balance in the direction of possibility and hope. He said you needed to do that when you believed in something. And maybe that's why, in the years ahead, I took particular delight in sending him emails from Turkey, Namibia, China, Brazil, Scotland, India—wherever I might be speaking or leading a workshop and people would tell me stories about their own White Ribbon Campaigns. Our little idea had spread around the world.

One of the things I always loved about Jack was that although he was great at trusting others to do their jobs and at assembling volunteers and supporters for his many causes, he also had a roll-up-his-sleeves quality. So let me end with a story about that, a story about Jack and Olivia, for it is really *their* story—as many of Jack's stories properly are.

Unknown to the voting public, Olivia and Jack shared a penchant for matchmaking. One summer's day in 1997 I got a call from Olivia more or less informing me that she was inviting herself over for dinner with a friend of hers, Betty Chee. She and Betty had been friends since they were teens. After dinner, Olivia wandered off for an in-depth look at my small garden and within a year Betty and I were living together, now friends with both Olivia and Jack.

Betty and I didn't see any reason to get officially married, but in 2001 we held a ceremony with family and friends to signify our commitment to each other. It was out back of our Victorian-era farmhouse near Kingston. There was no question about whom we'd ask to be master of ceremonies, for Jack was a man born for the job. But then, Olivia and Jack said they'd also like to look after the flowers. They arrived in a borrowed car the night before the ceremony. They refused help as they unloaded vases and huge bags of cut flowers into the garage. There was no room for volunteers, not because there was no physical space, but because it was as if they felt responsible for bringing us together and figured it was their responsibility to make at least this detail just right.

It had been a long day of preparations. Betty and I and the others who were staying with us went to bed at midnight or one. By then Jack and Olivia had made it to the stage of trimming all the flower stalks and putting them in big buckets of water. I don't know what time their labours ended—3 AM? 4 AM?—but I know they both worked late into the night under Olivia's artistic eye.

They were friends like that. And Jack was a man like that. Right out of a storybook. Tom Sawyer and a carefree rascal one minute, the Pied Piper and Robin Hood the next—not stealing from the rich, but at least saying that ours needed to be a far more caring society in which we politically *and* personally challenge the ever-widening gap between those who have money and power and those who do not. But more than anything, Jack was a loving brother, a brother-in-arms. A man with the greatest of hearts. A man who said if something needed to get done, we were damn well going to do it together.

Orange Pop and Paper Moustaches
JAMEY HEATH

I had not visited Parliament Hill for more than five years before the week of Jack's death. There, in almost the very spot on the lawn where he launched his campaign, were piles of flowers, handwritten notes, cans of orange pop, the odd paper moustache. A few days later, at City Hall in Toronto the evening before his funeral, I went to read the innumerable chalk farewells and to soak in the effect his life had had on the thousands of mourners.

One image that stands out is of two young men. They were not your typical lefty activist types. They looked as if, a few years earlier, they might have been good at high school sports. One was standing on the other's shoulders to reach a bit of concrete not yet chalked upon and to write another goodbye. I would not, I confess, have pegged them as NDP sympathizers—but there they were, on a Friday night, utterly sincere.

What was it about Jack that triggered such a geyser of emotion that week? In a time when politicians enjoy less and less respect, and politics is seen to create more problems than it solves, something transcended the cynicism. That something was Jack.

Come On, eh, Guys
RICHARD ZAJCHOWSKI

By the time we were fourteen years old, Jack and I had become accomplished competitive swimmers. We went to swim competitions in Ottawa and New England. On many of these trips we were billeted at the homes of members of the host swim club.

In early July of that year we went to a big swim meet in Gardner, Massachusetts. Jack, two teammates, and I were billeted together. One of our teammates had managed to buy a recent copy of *Playboy* magazine and brought it out for all of us to ogle. Being a very straight-laced young Catholic boy, I screwed up my courage and said, "Come on, eh, guys—don't do that." I refused to look at the magazine. I knew instantly that I would be subjected to considerable mockery, and I was. But I noticed that Jack wasn't joining in. He just looked pensively at me. Over the next few years I continued to repeat that phrase, "Come on, eh, guys—don't do that," whenever any of my teammates swore or used foul language. The phrase became one of my trademarks, but

Jack never joined in the inevitable mockery, any more than he had the first time.

Even the last time I saw him, six weeks before he died, Jack brought up how my phrase "Come on, eh, guys—don't do that" had taught him the importance of sticking up for what you believe in, even if it isn't welcomed.

Foiled!
JEAN CHAREST

I first met Jack through his father.

I had just been elected to Parliament in the 1984 election and was getting settled in my new office in the Confederation Building when I met Bob Layton. Even though I was his son's age, we soon became friends. I distinctly remember hearing him talk about his son with affection and admiration; he was a very proud father. In fact, two years before Bob Layton and I entered Parliament, Jack had already been elected to Toronto City Council. While Bob Layton did not always share his son's beliefs, he was one of Jack's biggest fans, so I had the opportunity to meet Jack on numerous occasions back then.

I enjoyed bringing up one event in particular when Jack was around. The story always gave us both a good laugh.

During the Progressive Conservative Party's 1993 leadership race, when I was the federal environment minister, I went to Toronto's Empire Club to deliver a speech. Bob Layton, who was caucus chair at the time, informed me that his son Jack planned to attend the press briefing following my speech to challenge me before the media on what he believed to be the government's lack of ambition on the issue of greenhouse-gas reduction. I imagine he would not have been too pleased to find out that his father had warned me about his intention to disrupt the briefing.

I had my eye on Jack the entire time. It was clear that he was preparing to step in. When I felt he was on the verge of speaking up, I pretended to have just noticed him. I stepped away from the microphone, went to shake his hand, and said, "Jack! So glad to see you! How are your parents? Please say hi to your mother for me." Visibly thrown off by the move, he did not have the chance to give me the documents he meant to hand over in front of the press. Thanks to his father, I had foiled his plan. Just a few months later, I admitted to Jack that his father had let me in on his intentions. From then on, we often reminisced about that day.

I will never forget Jack Layton. He was larger than life. A remarkable man. Someone who will continue to inspire us for many years to come.

An Ideal Political Opportunity
KARL BÉLANGER

The room was packed. The people were in a good mood. The man stood up and walked towards the front of the room. My wife looked over at me, a glimmer of concern in her eyes, but still smiling. I lowered my eyes, pretending to ignore what was happening. In any event, it was too late: two years earlier I had invited him, and now Jack was at my wedding, on the shore of Lac Leamy in Gatineau.

Full of emotion and personal and political anecdotes, his improvised speech lasted a good nine minutes—double that of the father of the bride! But you would never know it and our guests discovered at that moment what I had known for a long time: Jack Layton was a man of spirit—the same in front of and behind the camera, in private and in public life.

On January 25, 2003, the New Democrats elected Jack Layton leader of the party on the first ballot. I had been working for the outgoing leader, Alexa McDonough, since 1997 and, as a staffer, didn't take part in this leadership race. Concerned about the future of the party, I wandered through the corridors of the National Trade Centre in Toronto while Layton's supporters celebrated and the other sides rallied, drying their tears. It was then that I met the communications advisor for Jack Layton's campaign. "Your turn," he said. My turn? I didn't know Layton very well, even if we were part of the same team of candidates in the 1993 federal elections. (I ran in Jonquière while he ran in Rosedale.) Later that night, I was officially asked to become a member of the transition team and to organize the first press conference for the new NDP leader, the very next day. This transition would become an eight-and-a-half-year journey.

From the beginning, Jack Layton was a challenge for the communications team. Here was a municipal politician, a former university professor, not very well known outside Toronto, arriving in Ottawa, in the big leagues of Canadian politics. His reflexes were those of a man of the people, a community approach. At ease in front of the cameras, he had a tendency to want to explain and demonstrate, to become "Professor Jack," which too often led him where he shouldn't go, particularly into the imaginary world created by hypothetical questions of journalists of the Parliamentary Press Gallery. Also, this Torontonian, born in Montreal, was a Canadian partisan, which isn't ideal for getting through to Toronto. What to do?

Despite all his experience, Jack Layton understood that he had a lot to learn if he wanted to achieve his ultimate goal: to become the next prime minister of Canada and to make it a fairer, more equitable country. His ambition was not personal but collective. He had a thirst for learning, understanding, self-improvement, and credibility. Tirelessly, we worked together to perfect his French, sharpen his instincts, and temper his anger and his enthusiasm. He learned to be disciplined, to end press statements when I announced the last question despite his temptation to continue. He and I developed multiple codes, and when I sent three quick messages to his BlackBerry, he knew he had to end a speech that was dragging on too long. That's why, to say goodbye, I gave three little knocks to his coffin as he lay in state in the foyer of the House.

Originally from Quebec, he was obsessed with the NDP's successive failures in his native province. Very early on, I understood there was a connection between Jack Layton and Quebecers. We had to take advantage of it. In September 2004, I jumped on an invitation from Radio-Canada's *Tout le monde en parle*, then in its first season. Despite the scepticism of my Anglophone colleagues with regard to this controversial show, with no equivalent in English Canada, we ploughed ahead. It was dangerous: Jack Layton had left Quebec more than twenty years earlier, his French was rusty, and despite the interest he had in Quebec culture, his points of reference dated back to another era.

Even so, we took the train to Montreal, where I presented to him in detail the profiles of the performers and guests and filled him in on current sociocultural events, to prepare him as best as possible to face this city and its questions. It worked. After that, we always accepted the invitations of Guy A. Lepage and his team. The repercussions of this first appearance were powerful: it was the beginning of a beautiful relationship between Quebecers and Jack.

In a number of interviews, press statements, and speeches, Jack Layton made himself known. And clearly, he was worth knowing. The man learned from his mistakes and gained in maturity over the years. He even ended up being an artist of Question Period on sitting days—he had not been comfortable in this parliamentary forum when he arrived, preferring negotiations and compromises to purely partisan confrontation, a practice inherited from his time in the municipal world.

Jack Layton truly saw the world in a positive way. His smile was sincere, his love of life contagious. For him, life was politics. He did politics with a smile, naturally. With hope. With optimism. With the profound conviction that, yes, it was possible, we could do better. Jack Layton marked his era by remaining himself and respecting the advice that his father had once given him: never miss an opportunity to serve. No, Jack didn't miss it. All of Canada is thankful for that.

From Sceptic to Believer
PEGGY NASH

The things that impressed me about Jack Layton were his optimism and his capacity for hard work. Problems didn't seem to get him down or make him cynical; they were a source of creativity and activism. This quality was sorely needed at that moment, as there was a lot of cynicism and many were really down on the NDP.

Shortly after Jack became leader of the party in 2003, he was invited to a dinner in Ottawa with the executive of the Canadian Labour Congress. As a long-time member of the executive, I was very familiar with the tensions not only between the various unions but also between labour generally and the NDP. Frankly, optimism was in short supply. In his speech to the small group of labour leaders gathered at the dinner, Jack painted his vision for building the party, organizing, and winning more and more seats, even in Quebec. There was polite applause and sceptical looks exchanged across the room. Yeah, sure, we're on the move. Uh-huh, we're going to win lots of seats from the Liberals and the Conservatives in Quebec.

The new leader represented a fresh start, but not everyone there really knew him. Understandably, some saw him as disconnected from the labour movement. Jack's background was in city politics, and he had championed many important issues from cycling to ending violence against women to greening the economy. There needed to be a period of relationship building with labour leaders. With typical gusto, Jack launched tirelessly into this work. He went around the room and spent time with each person. He would later follow up with individual meetings and became a frequent voice on the other end of their phones, whether they wanted him there or not.

But that evening, when Jack came to our table, he pulled a chair over to have a private conversation with me. It was there that he first approached me about running for federal office. I was polite but less than receptive. Why would I, as a senior person in the Canadian Auto Workers union with the freedom to work on many issues I cared strongly about, throw all of that aside for a rump party of thirteen seats, with little money and not much chance of success?

"We are going to change politics in the country," he said. "I need you to be part of it. Women look up to you; you're a respected national labour leader. You can play a key role in shaping the future of Canada." It's flattering to be asked to run, but I felt it was madness. The party wasn't very strong, I already had a key role in my union, and I had no experience in running for public office. I politely declined.

The idea kept rumbling around in my mind, and every so often I would re-examine it and challenge myself. Some months later, CAW president Buzz Hargrove invited Jack to the National Executive Board meeting in Port Elgin, Ontario, three hours northwest of Toronto. Again he was full of optimism and buzzing with energy. The leaders at the executive meeting were friendly and positive, but it was still very much a "show me" period of Jack's leadership. He was still untested.

His schedule was very tight and he had to leave right after his speech to return to Toronto. Since Jack didn't drive, the union sent a car to get him to and from the meeting. I also had to return to Toronto, so rather than drive myself I hitched a ride with Jack. During the drive he was continually on the phone, returning emails, getting things done. Still, he took the opportunity to press me again on the idea of running for the party. By then I had done a lot of thinking and was more open to the idea. He made the work sound so exciting—because for him, it *was* exciting. He spoke of the thrill of building support and campaigning, of winning office and getting results.

His passion for progressive change, his commitment, and his complete devotion to the cause of public life inspired me. This was what I lived for. While I didn't commit to Jack during that trip, in my own mind I knew I was on the road to making the decision to run for office. I imagined the thousands of such conversations that Jack must have had over his career, inspiring and cajoling and persuading people to take the plunge. His energy inspired me to rise to the occasion, and I have never regretted it.

O Canada
DI McINTYRE

Our grandparents and parents always expected us to stand respectfully and sing "O Canada" whenever and wherever it was played. Even at the beginning of a hockey game, we all would stand at attention in front of the television to sing our national anthem. "O Canada" has always moved me—it makes me think of my grandmother standing straight and still and singing. I also think of our great fortune to have been born Canadian, and of all the benefits that this geographical good fortune has given us. I remember being particularly moved one day at the University of Ottawa, standing between Jack and Stephen Lewis, thinking about how much these two men had done to stand on guard for all of us. During our last conversation, Jack said that soon he'd be standing next to his dad proudly singing "O Canada" again.

In 2003, I gave a copy of Great-Grandfather Layton's "Dominion March" to Gordon Slater, then Dominion carillonneur, suggesting that it would be great to play this when Jack became prime minister. Instead, the march was adapted by Slater's successor, Andrea McReady, and played on the carillon as Jack's casket left Parliament Hill in 2011. Few would have known what was being played, but for members of the Layton family this was a very moving tribute.

Proof Positive
TERRY GRIER

There was always something exceptional about Jack Layton. He had an infectious optimism, grounded in an intuitively cool assessment of facts and possibilities, that inspired hope and confidence that even the direst situation could be overcome. You came away from being with Jack buoyed up and feeling better about your chances. This combined with a palpable energy that radiated from him almost like a force field.

In 1974 I was involved in hiring Jack Layton onto the faculty of our politics department at Ryerson. He was one of two very qualified candidates. What tipped the balance in his favour was his sunny, confident, enthusiastic, energetic personality. You knew right away that he would be a compelling teacher. He spent more than ten years at Ryerson, an extremely successful and popular professor, and while carrying a full teaching load completed his PhD in political economy. At McGill Jack had been enormously influenced by political philosopher and New Democrat Charles Taylor, and he already carried with him a strong commitment to social and economic justice. It was this that made him decide, after some years, to run for Toronto City Council.

In his early years on Council Jack struck some as too brash and cocky, a know-it-all who always had an answer. It's true there was never anything diffident about Jack, but this was not arrogance or showing off. This was an early, still unpolished manifestation of his impatience with self-serving politics and his burning desire to right wrongs. In my eyes it was a virtue. By the time his long career in municipal politics was over, the mature Jack Layton had acquired a remarkable skill at building coalitions among colleagues with differing points of view to enact practical solutions to people's real problems.

There was never any malice in Jack. He liked people and got on well with colleagues and opponents of all stripes. He held strongly to his basic beliefs, but he was never dogmatic. For him politics was an arena in which to find answers and make good things happen, not a platform for preaching political ideology.

A Search for Meaning
JOE MIHEVC

The week Jack died was one of the most profound and moving I have experienced at Toronto City Hall. Like so many, I found myself often in tears, hugging friends, telling Jack stories, still in shock that a friend had died too young, in the middle of his contribution to our city and country. My family spent a full day in Nathan Phillips Square, reading the thousands of chalk messages and art, walking, thinking, remembering, and visiting with all kinds of people. I think we all were trying to find the meaning in Jack's passing and the public response, what it meant for us personally, socially, politically, and spiritually.

Although I did not have a conversation with him about religion, spirituality, or values, I knew Jack to be a very spiritual person. It was the work that revealed the values and inspiration. Jack used his power to create a better Canada and Toronto for all, but especially for people who are on the margins, who are suffering, and who need support. This appealed to me and perhaps was why I found in Jack a kindred spirit. I have always been attracted to the insights of liberation theology in developing countries and the way this religious movement within Christianity placed the struggles and suffering of the poor at the centre of the faith community's reflection and action. In the language of liberation theology, Jack lived the "preferential option for the poor." Struggling with those on the margins informed his thinking, his action, and his life commitment.

Every so often, history gives us people who show us a way to be fully human and fully alive. They show us that compassion and social justice can happen right now and right here. I daresay that for Canadians, Jack was one such leader. Jack was certainly not a religious leader; nevertheless, I do think that the life and commitments that Jack displayed revealed a sense of spirituality and deep human values.

Jack's last letter to Canadians embodies the political and, indeed, spiritual ideals for which we will strive. We will tell his story to our children and our grandchildren. We will sing Jack's words, "So let us be loving, hopeful and optimistic. And we'll change the world."

Jack's service was so moving: yes, it was the words people said and the singing, but also *who* said the words and sang the songs—a gay priest backed by a gay and lesbian choir, an indigenous chief, a disabled man calling us in French to believe in a better tomorrow and calling Jack brother, and a Muslim sister and Jewish brother linked in prayer. These people, too often shunned in our society, were all there, front and centre, grieving Jack's loss while celebrating the values of inclusion and social solidarity.

Jack was a master with a great sense of political timing. His death came just as many of us were wondering whether Torontonians and Canadians were abandoning our commitments to that deeply Canadian sense of social solidarity. The political climate seemed to be heading in the opposite direction: just worry about Number One; don't pay taxes; if you need something, pay for it or you don't get it; keep out the immigrants—they are not like us; shut libraries: if you want a book, go buy it.

The timing of Jack's death sowed a renewal of the hope that we could build a better Toronto and a better Canada. The tears and gatherings and remembrances and chalk art helped people reaffirm that the community-building social struggle was wholly worthwhile.

Jack's life and death taught us not to despair, not to lose hope. One of the most profound things he said to Reverend Brent Hawkes in the days before his death was, "How I live my life every day is an act of worship." Every act of social solidarity, of working to build a better world, is a prayer. Jack showed us that it is possible, each in our own way, to live such a life.

The last page of the order of service at Jack's funeral was left blank. The previous page read, "Use this space to write something you will do to make our world a better place." This too was so characteristic of Jack, who often proclaimed, "Never leave a meeting without an action strategy."

If Jack's life and death have meaning for us, it is for all of us to reconfirm that a great life is one in which we struggle for justice, in which we live a life of courage and compassion, always bringing those who are excluded into the centre of our thoughts and actions.

Grace
DI McINTYRE

In September 2006, Jack brought home a gift that Peter Julian had presented "with respect and thanks to our leader Jack Layton." It is a framed watercolour of the Prairies with a J. S. Woodsworth grace that summed up Jack's outlook on our blessings and on our responsibilities as occupants of this shared universe:

> *We are thankful for these and all of the good things of life.*
> *We recognize that they are part of our common heritage and come to us through the efforts of our brothers and sisters the world over.*
> *What we desire for ourselves, we wish for all.*
> *To this end, may we take our share in the world's work and the world's struggles.*

The gift is framed in hundred-year-old reclaimed Douglas fir. A peaceful reminder of both Jack and about what matters in life, it graces my kitchen.

Love, Jack
PETER EHRLICH

Jack signed off every correspondence in one of two ways, either "My best wishes always" or "Love, Jack." Neither was reserved for me, I assure you. Mahatma Gandhi once said, "Love takes courage." If that's the case, Jack was the most courageous man in politics and life. He never hesitated to tell you that he loved you.

A Gift

MINERVA HUI (*with thanks to* VIVIAN KONG)

Jack was starting his battle with cancer when my husband Brian was ending his. They had connected in so many ways that a very deep friendship developed in their short time together—both grew up in Montreal, resettled in Ontario, were passionately involved in their communities, and revelled in each other's wicked sense of humour. When Jack met Brian's son, he praised Brian's work in the community by saying, "You know, your dad's a real shit disturber." After Jack's cancer diagnosis, Brian told him, "Well, it looks like we got ourselves in some trouble, didn't we?"

After Brian passed away in the spring of 2010, I wrote to Jack thanking him for his calls and visits. Those simple gestures had greatly lifted Brian's spirits. I also let Jack know that his touching statement in the House of Commons in remembrance of Brian had enlightened a dark and trying time. It was an unexpected gift that helped the family heal from the terrible wounds the government had inflicted on them when Brian blew the whistle on CSIS.

That summer, Jack invited me to his home for coffee. He wanted me to see the Canadian flag his family had given to him as a birthday present. I arrived to a warm greeting from Jack and a house humming with the morning energy of people getting ready for the day. Olivia was having breakfast while going over the newspaper as her mom was tidying up. Jack got us our coffee and we headed to the front porch to enjoy the beautiful summer day and gaze on that flag. Brian and I had received a complimentary flag from our constituency office; it hung in front of our house for years and he loved to watch the maple leaf waving from the window of our living room. Jack told me that his flag was being flown in Brian's memory.

I brought along a book that Brian wanted Jack to have, a book about musicians and their guitars—a fitting gift to a man who loved music and played the guitar. Brian hadn't given the book to Jack because he saw that the book was autographed with a note to him. He was so disappointed. When I told Jack about this and how Brian really wanted Jack to have something from him, Jack opened the book and brushed his hand over the note back and forth while whispering, "Oh Brian. Dear Brian." We both wept, and allowed ourselves the luxury of being sad for a while.

I will never forget Jack's incredible capacity for generosity, kindness, and compassion. I cannot imagine how difficult it must have been for him to reach out so often to us while he himself was starting his own battle with cancer. Even though he lost this battle, he remained optimistic to the end, leaving the country with a message of hope. For me, after seeing him in such a state of sadness, his words of optimism were even more poignant.

Across the Aisle
BILL FREEMAN

After Jack's death, politicians and thousands of others expressed their admiration and respect for him. He had touched people with his generosity and commitment. More than anything, it was the warmth of his personality and his optimism that had moved people, but there was one other thing that was said about him: he had helped to change the way politics was practised in Ottawa. I was not surprised.

Curiously, in all of the tributes to Jack after he died, I found the comments of Stephen Harper among the most moving. In the House of Commons he said, "One of the pleasures of serving in this place is the friendships that develop and sometimes the surprise of friendships that grow between opponents, the affections that develop in spite of our strongest partisan instincts."

The prime minister was speaking of Jack as a friend. Harper is a man, we are told, who does not make friends easily. He is remote and almost isolated, at times ruthless in his partisanship. And yet he had come to consider Jack Layton a friend, a relationship that even many of Harper's closest allies could not claim. That was Jack's gift, and we are all better for it.

Dancing Under the Stars
SVEND ROBINSON

Jack and Olivia loved the Gulf Islands, off the coast of British Columbia, where my partner Max and I have had a house for more than a decade. They visited many times, staying in the house and enjoying the beauty and tranquility of Galiano and Parker islands. Jack and I enjoyed kayaking the waters around Galiano, and he and I had many trips together around the islands. He also enjoyed paddling with Olivia. As well, at least once they flew out with their famous tandem bicycle and brought it over to Galiano Island, amazingly travelling the many hills and valleys on the island with ease.

Jack loved to take our motorboat, a seventeen-foot Carolina skiff, on runs from Galiano to nearby Salt Spring Island, especially on Saturday mornings to visit the wonderful outdoor market there. His good friend from Toronto, George Ehring, lives on the island and was a trustee representing Salt Spring for many years; Jack loved to visit with George and talk politics and the old days in Toronto with him. Olivia set up her bamboo easel on the deck and painted several special works looking out over the mountains and ocean, one of which has a place of honour still today at our Galiano house.

When Jack took the helm of the motorboat he always ran it flat out as we sped across the waters of Trincomali Sound, with him standing behind the wheel, his hair blowing in the wind, and me sitting up front keeping an eye out for deadheads and rocks. But he knew the route well and never grounded the boat. On one occasion, though, we had stopped mid-route to have a look at some seals playing nearby. When he revved up the motor to move us forward again, he caught me off guard and sent me flying into the drink, then roared with laughter as I climbed soaking wet into the boat. Another time we ran out of gas and the two of us had to paddle a long distance to Ganges harbour on Salt Spring. Jack tried to persuade me that this was great exercise.

Jack wrote many chapters of both of his books at our places on Galiano and Parker, acknowledging this in the forewords, and at one point came close to buying a beautiful piece of land on Parker only to find that it had been sold the week before after having been on the market for a couple of years. He and Olivia loved the islands and he often told me that he found the beauty, serenity, and peace of the island very healing from the bruising battles of politics. They were great cooks and craved the delicious Dungeness crabs that we would catch after Max loaded the traps with fish he had caught earlier.

One of my favourite images of Jack and Olivia is of the

two of them dancing arm in arm on a starlit night on the deck of our house at Galiano, with a neighbour couple with whom they had shared a great evening of wine, good food, laughter, and music. They drew strength, peace, and energy from the beauty of the islands. It still pains me terribly as I paddle those waters today to know that Jack will not be there to share this special place that he and Olivia both loved.

Hamba Gahle, *Jack Layton!*
ANVER SALOOJEE

Jack Layton completed his PhD coursework at York University in 1974, and that year he joined Ryerson Polytechnical Institute's department of politics and School of Public Administration. Three years later, in September 1977, I joined Ryerson's sociology department as a sessional instructor. I was immediately introduced to Jack by one of my mentors, Professor Solly Patel, chair of the department of politics.

In his open and gregarious manner, Jack immediately took me under his wing and invited me to his classes so I could get a sense of what teaching at Ryerson entailed. A number of things impressed me about Jack's approach to pedagogy. His classroom was an experiment in learning, it was energetic, and it engaged every student in both the learning and the teaching.

For Jack, the students in his class were partners in politics—not just in the theory of political science but also in the practice of politics. All political views and ideas were entertained; students were encouraged to voice their opinions and to respectfully contest the ideas of others. In class Jack was not simply the teacher; he was the conductor of a symphony of ideas, of contesting ideologies, and of political engagement.

At the end of one class Jack and I went out for coffee. In discussing the class, I received from Jack what I consider the golden nugget of pedagogy. "Remember," Jack said, "teaching is a privilege. No other profession allows us to engage with so many learners over a prolonged period where they look to us for answers. Don't give them the answers—help them develop the capacity to find the answers themselves."

From this I took a number of key lessons about the teaching and learning project. For Jack it was about respecting the views of all learners, validating them as learners. It was not about imposing one's views on learners but about facilitating discussion and dialogue. It was about faculty members not violating their position of trust and it was about empowering learners to set and achieve their own learning goals. In short, for Jack, it was about creating a respectful but dynamic and inclusive teaching and learning environment in which all students could develop their talents and capacities. What more could a budding academic ask for?

Beyond the classroom I gained more insights into Jack as he practised politics. Certainly he was as passionate about politics in the city of Toronto as I was about ending apartheid in South Africa. Jack was committed to both. He was an ardent supporter of the anti-apartheid movement, of the struggle of the Chilean community against the military junta in Chile, of the Tamils who fled Sri Lanka, and of all peoples who came to Toronto as refugees fleeing oppression. In this Jack was both a deeply committed nationalist and an internationalist. He was as concerned about domestic politics as he was about local politics.

The concern with the plight of others would pay great

dividends as Jack moved from teaching politics to becoming a politician. Volunteers from incredibly diverse communities gave selflessly of their time and resources to help Jack get elected—first as a Toronto councillor in 1982, when he upset the incumbent, Gordon Chong, and again in February 1991, when he became the first official NDP candidate for the mayoralty in a race that pitted him against Mayor Art Eggleton. Eggleton pulled out of the race, but Jack eventually lost the mayoralty to June Rowlands. Jack had successfully galvanized a rainbow coalition of volunteers—they were the face of a new Toronto demanding their rightful place in the politics of their city. And Jack, much as he did in his classroom, gave them a voice and legitimated their voices.

A few months after losing the mayoralty race, Jack held a fundraiser to deal with the campaign debt he had incurred. Once again, the incredible diversity of Toronto was on display as Torontonians from different backgrounds came out to help Jack as he helped them. At the event Jack displayed his wonderful auctioneering skills.

Right after the fundraising event, my partner, Zuby, who was working for a community-based agency, approached Jack for assistance with fundraising for the agency. True to form, Jack gave unstintingly of his time and ideas. He opened his door to Zuby and the agency. Such was Jack—he was totally unselfish. He was unselfish when he shared his approach to pedagogy with a first-year academic, he was unselfish when he supported those fighting injustices globally, and he was just as unselfish with a locally based community agency.

The tie that binds these seemingly disparate events is Jack as the quintessential organic intellectual who leads by example, gives voice to the voiceless, eschews dogma, speaks truth to power, and effectively combines theory and practice. Without a doubt, Jack remains an organic intellectual and a public intellectual. Borrowing a phrase from South Africa, where people who wish to remember those who made the supreme sacrifice in the fight against apartheid say *Hamba Gahle*, I too say *Hamba Gahle, Jack. Go well, go in peace.*

"How I Live My Life Every Day"
BRENT HAWKES

I usually go to Roy Thomson Hall on Christmas Eve, when the Metropolitan Community Church of Toronto celebrates its annual Christmas Eve Service. Jack and Olivia had been attending this service for a number of years. Normally, I look up in the balcony to see Jack and Olivia sitting there. Normally, I greet them outside in the hall with their Santa Claus hats on. But on August 27, 2011, it was different. We had come together to celebrate Jack's life and mourn his passing.

I had met with Jack and Olivia on several occasions leading up to his passing, and cherish those times so very much. Jack shared with me what was dearest to his heart. He said that he was very, very grateful. He felt very blessed to have lived so long, very blessed to have met and worked with so many wonderful people. He felt inspired by his fellow Canadians, particularly by young people, and he was in awe at the trust given to him. He talked about his love for his family, and for Olivia. He loved and respected Olivia. He admired her wisdom and strength, and described her as his rock in life. And while Jack was very grateful about his life, he was sad that he did not have more time. More time to continue and improve things—a movement towards a better Canada.

Jack believed that Canada was a great country and yet he was very clear that there's a lot of work remaining to be done. We are a people coming from different places with different beliefs and different approaches. And yet we can be one, working together for a better Canada. He wanted us to inspire and challenge each other as individuals and—this was very important to Jack—work together in partnership. Jack's goal in life was to bring people together: young and old, diverse voices, different perspectives, and opposing beliefs. Jack was a spiritual person. He didn't wear it on his sleeve, but in one of our conversations, he said to me, "Brent, I believe how I live my life every day is my act of worship."

Jack's life inspired us all. Jack left a lasting impression on this country. Long after the talking is done, and long after all those expressions of deep love and admiration written in chalk on the concrete at City Hall have washed off, the legacy of Jack Layton will not be in how much power we have, it will be in how all of us exercise our personal power for a better world. It will be in our actions and how we take those actions together. If the Olympics made us prouder Canadians, Jack's life made us better Canadians. I happen to be in the business of believing in miracles. We can be a better people, for in Jack Layton we've seen how to try.

A Letter to Canadians

August 20, 2011
Toronto, Ontario

Dear Friends,

Tens of thousands of Canadians have written to me in recent weeks to wish me well. I want to thank each and every one of you for your thoughtful, inspiring and often beautiful notes, cards and gifts. Your spirit and love have lit up my home, my spirit, and my determination.

Unfortunately my treatment has not worked out as I hoped. So I am giving this letter to my partner Olivia to share with you in the circumstance in which I cannot continue.

I recommend that Hull–Aylmer MP Nycole Turmel continue her work as our interim leader until a permanent successor is elected.

I recommend the party hold a leadership vote as early as possible in the New Year, on approximately the same time-lines as in 2003, so that our new leader has ample time to reconsolidate our team, renew our party and our program, and move forward towards the next election.

A few additional thoughts:

To other Canadians who are on journeys to defeat cancer and to live their lives, I say this: please don't be discouraged that my own journey hasn't gone as well as I had hoped. You must not lose your own hope. Treatments and therapies have never been better in the face of this disease. You have every reason to be optimistic, determined, and focused on the future. My only other advice is to cherish every moment with those you love at every stage of your journey, as I have done this summer.

To the members of my party: we've done remarkable things together in the past eight years. It has been a privilege to lead the New Democratic Party and I am most grateful for your confidence, your support, and the endless hours of volunteer commitment you have devoted to our cause. There will be those who will try to persuade you to give up our cause. But that cause is much bigger than any one leader. Answer them by recommitting with energy and determination to our work. Remember our proud history of social justice, universal health care, public pensions and making sure no one is left behind. Let's continue to move forward. Let's demonstrate in everything we do in the four years before us that we are ready to serve our beloved Canada as its next government.

To the members of our parliamentary caucus: I have been privileged to work with each and every one of you. Our caucus meetings were always the highlight of my week. It has been my role to ask a great deal from you. And now I am going to do so again. Canadians will be closely watching you in the months to come. Colleagues, I know you will make the tens of thousands of members of our party proud of you by demonstrating the same seamless teamwork and solidarity that has earned us the confidence of millions of Canadians in the recent election.

To my fellow Quebecers: On May 2nd, you made an historic decision. You decided that the way to replace Canada's Conservative federal government with something better was by working together in partnership with progressive-minded Canadians across the country. You made the right decision then; it is still the right decision today; and it will be the right decision right through to the next election, when we will succeed, together. You have elected a superb team of New Democrats to Parliament. They are going to be doing remarkable things in the years to come to make this country better for us all.

To young Canadians: All my life I have worked to make things better. Hope and optimism have defined my political career, and I continue to be hopeful and optimistic about Canada. Young people have been a great source of inspiration for me. I have met and talked with so many of you about your dreams, your frustrations, and your ideas for change. More and more, you are engaging in politics because you want to change things for the better. Many of you have placed your trust in our party. As my time in political life draws to a close I want to share with you my belief in your power to change this country and this world. There are great challenges before you, from the overwhelming nature of climate change to the unfairness of an economy that excludes so many from our collective wealth, and the changes necessary to build a more inclusive and generous Canada. I believe in you. Your energy, your vision, your passion for justice are exactly what this country needs today. You need to be at the heart of our economy, our political life, and our plans for the present and the future.

And finally, to all Canadians: Canada is a great country, one of the hopes of the world. We can be a better one—a country of greater equality, justice, and opportunity. We can build a prosperous economy and a society that shares its benefits more fairly. We can look after our seniors. We can offer better futures for our children. We can do our part to save the world's environment. We can restore our good name in the world. We can do all of these things because we finally have a party system at the national level where there are real choices; where your vote matters; where working for change can actually bring about change. In the months and years to come, New Democrats will put a compelling new alternative to you. My colleagues in our party are an impressive, committed team. Give them a careful hearing; consider the alternatives; and consider that we can be a better, fairer, more equal country by working together. Don't let them tell you it can't be done.

My friends, love is better than anger. Hope is better than fear. Optimism is better than despair. So let us be loving, hopeful and optimistic. And we'll change the world.

All my very best,

Jack Layton

Acknowledgements

We would like to thank all the contributors, whose reminiscences and photos form the body of this book. They are proof that the old adage is true: "If you want something done, ask a busy person." These people are all very busy indeed, yet they kindly took the time to share their thoughts and memories with us. We also want to express our gratitude to Nathan Rotman and Olivia Chow, who helped us immensely in identifying and contacting potential contributors.

We would also like to thank our editors, Bob Chodos and Ginny Freeman MacOwan, who worked their magic on the manuscript. Thanks as well to Publisher Jim Lorimer, Editorial Director Diane Young, and Production Editor Amanda Lucier for their support, encouragement, and great patience.

A Chronology of Jack's Life

EARLY YEARS (1950–1964)

- Born John Gilbert "Jack" Layton on July 18, 1950, in Montreal, Quebec
- Raised in Hudson, Quebec
- Parents are Doris Elizabeth Steeves, a grand-niece of William Steeves (a Father of Confederation), and Robert Layton (a former Conservative MP and Cabinet Minister). Jack's grandfather, Gilbert Layton, was a member of Quebec's Legislative Assembly for Maurice Duplessis's Union Nationale

HIGH SCHOOL YEARS (1964–1967)

- Attended Hudson High School
- President of Hudson Student Council 1966–7
- Graduated 1967

UNIVERSITY YEARS (1968–1983)

- Attended McGill University as an undergraduate
- Prime Minister of the Quebec Youth Parliament 1969–70
- Married Sally Halford in 1969; this marriage produced two children, Michael and Sarah; Jack and Sally were divorced in 1983
- Received a BA in Political Science from McGill in 1970
- Attended York University as a graduate student
- Received a MA in Political Science in 1971
- Received a PhD in Political Science in 1983

TEACHING CAREER (1974 ON)

- Taught at Ryerson Polytechnical Institute from 1974 on
- Taught at University of Toronto (Adjunct Professor, Geography,

Planning Programme, and teaching appointment with Innis
College, University of Toronto, Environmental Studies)
- York University (Fellow, Calumet College)

YEARS AS A MUNICIPAL POLITICIAN (1982–2003)
- Served as a City of Toronto Councillor from 1982–1991 and
  from 1997–2003
- Met Olivia Chow when he was an auctioneer for an event
  at the Village Green and she was a Cantonese interpreter in
  1985; they were married in 1988
- Served as a Metro Toronto Councillor from 1985–1988 and
  from 1994–1997
- Served as deputy mayor of the City of Toronto in 1990
- Ran for mayor of Toronto in 1991, but lost to June Rowlands
- Published *Homelessness: The Making and Unmaking of a Crisis*
  in 2000
- Became President of the Federation of Canadian
  Municipalities in 2001
- Served as Chair of the Toronto Board of Health; Chair of the
  Economic Development and Planning Committee of Metro
  Toronto; Chair of Metropolitan Toronto's Planning and
  Transportation Committee; Chair of Advisory Committee on
  Homeless and Socially Isolated Persons; board member for the
  Toronto Port Authority; federal board member of the Climate
  Change Protection Program
- Published *Speaking Out: Ideas that Work for Canadians* in 2004

YEARS AS A FEDERAL POLITICIAN (2003–2011)
- Leader of the NDP from 2003 to 2011
- Member of Parliament from 2004 to 2011

Contributors

SHAWN A-IN-CHUT ATLEO is the national chief of the Assembly of First Nations.

NICOLAS-DOMINIC AUDET is the former NDP Quebec section director and currently works for the Office of the Official Opposition.

SUSAN BAKER is executive director of the Riverdale Share Community Association and producer of the Riverdale Share Concert.

RICHARD BARRY was Jack Layton's executive assistant at Toronto City Hall and during Jack's tenure as president of the Federation of Canadian Municipalities. He is the former executive director of the White Ribbon Campaign, and is currently an Ontario civil servant and musician.

PAUL J. BEDFORD is the former Toronto chief planner.

KARL BÉLANGER is the principal secretary to the Leader of Canada's Official Opposition, Tom Mulcair. He served as senior press secretary to Jack Layton for eight years and, in that capacity, he facilitated Layton's very first and his very last press conferences as Leader of the New Democratic Party of Canada.

DAVID V. J. BELL is a professor emeritus, senior scholar, and former dean of the Faculty of Environmental Studies, York University.

BILL BLAIKIE was an NDP MP from 1979 to 2008. He served in Parliament with Jack Layton from 2004 to 2008, and from 1984 to 1993 with Jack's father, Robert Layton.

REBECCA BLAIKIE is the national president of the NDP.

WILLY BLOMME is currently pursuing her doctoral degree at Johns Hopkins University. She worked as the volunteer coordinator on Jack Layton's NDP leadership campaign and as Layton's speechwriter from 2006 to 2008.

ED BROADBENT was leader of the federal New Democratic Party from 1975 to 1989. He returned to politics in 2004 to win a seat as an MP from Ottawa Centre. In 1993, he was made an Officer of the Order of Canada and was promoted to Companion in 2001.

JEAN CHAREST is premier of Quebec.

KEVIN CHIEF is the MLA for Point Douglas, Manitoba.

MARILYN CHURLEY is an Ontario Justice of the Peace and former Toronto city councillor and MPP. She was the national co-chair of Jack's 2002–2003 NDP Leadership Campaign.

PAUL COPELAND is a lawyer who practises criminal and national security law in Toronto.

CATHY CROWE is a street nurse.

LIBBY DAVIES is the NDP deputy leader and MP for Vancouver East.

PETER EHRLICH was responsible for marketing the White Ribbon Campaign for a number of years starting in 1990 while Jack Layton was chair, and served as his constituency assistant at Toronto City Hall from 1999 to 2001.

DEBBIE FIELD is executive director of FoodShare Toronto.

TIM FLANNERY is Australia's chief climate commissioner and author of *The Weather Makers*. His latest book is *Here on Earth: An Argument for Hope*.

BILL FREEMAN is a writer and community activist who lives on Toronto Island, a community where Jack and Olivia were married and often returned for support and spiritual renewal.

ANNE GOLDEN is president and CEO of the Conference Board of Canada.

MICHAEL GOLDRICK is an academic activist who special-
ized in urban life as an elected councillor, a community
organizer, and a professor of politics.

TERRY GRIER is president emeritus of Ryerson University
and a former MP. He was chair of the NDP's election-
planning committee throughout the Broadbent years.

NEIL HARTLING, author, river guide, and outfitter, makes
his home in Whitehorse, Yukon, where he operates
expeditions across the north on some of the most dramatic
rivers in the world. Neil says that people will protect what
they love, and so his successful business is a platform for
conservation and a labour of love.

FRANZ HARTMANN is executive director of the Toronto
Environmental Alliance.

BRENT HAWKES is senior pastor at the Metropolitan
Community Church of Toronto.

JAMEY HEATH was Jack Layton's communications director from 2002 to 2006.

MINERVA HUI and BRIAN McINNIS approached Jack as
their MP in 2005 because non-profits were facing unfair
federal cuts. At the time, Minerva was the Executive
Director of one of the non-profits slated for cuts. After
saving the agencies from shutting down, Minerva and
Brian worked in a variety of capacities in the NDP.

E. T. JACKSON is an Ottawa-based professor, consultant,
and author.

MICHAEL KAUFMAN is an educator and writer focused
on engaging men and boys to promote gender equality
and end violence against women. He works internation-
ally with the United Nations, NGOs, and governments,
and is the co-founder of the White Ribbon Campaign.

BRAD LAVIGNE served as an advisor to Jack for ten years.
He worked on Jack's leadership campaign in 2002, served

as communications director of the Party and the Caucus, national director of the Party, 2011 national Campaign Director and Jack's principal secretary.

DORIS LAYTON is Jack's mother.

NANCY LAYTON is Jack's sister.

SARAH LAYTON, Jack's daughter, is volunteer coordinator for the Stephen Lewis Foundation.

DEREK LEEBOSH is vice president, public affairs at Environics Research Group in Toronto.

ANNE McGRATH served as Chief of Staff to Jack Layton (2008–11), interim leader Nycole Turmel, and Thomas Mulcair. Anne was President of the NDP from 2006 until 2009 and served as National Equality Director for the Canadian Union of Public Employees.

DI McINTYRE is Jack's cousin and led his at-home Ottawa support team.

JOE MIHEVC is Toronto city councillor for St. Paul's.

PAUL MOIST is national president of the Canadian Union of Public Employees.

PEGGY NASH is member of Parliament for Parkdale–High Park.

MICHAEL P. O'HARA is a filmmaker and works in NABET 700, the union of Toronto film and television technicians.

BRIAN O'KEEFE is the former Secretary-Treasurer of CUPE Ontario and Co-Chair of the OMERS Sponsors Corporation.

JOHN PIPER is a long-time family friend and colleague in building community.

DICK PROCTOR was chair of the federal NDP caucus from 1998 to 2004. Jack Layton chose Proctor as his interim chief of staff in 2004 and acting federal party secretary in 2008.

DAVID RAESIDE is a professor of political science and sexual diversity studies at the University of Toronto.

ANVER SALOOJEE is president of the Faculty Association and a professor in the Department of Politics and School of Public Administration at Ryerson University.

SVEND ROBINSON was a New Democrat MP from 1979–2004. Currently, he lives in Switzerland where he coordinates parliamentary relations for The Global Fund to Fight AIDS, TB, and Malaria.

MYER SIEMIATYCKI is a professor of politics at Ryerson University.

KEVIN SYLVESTER is a broadcaster, author, and illustrator.

PETER TABUNS is an MPP and was Jack Layton's climate advisor during Jack's first year's on Parliament Hill.

BRIAN TOPP is executive director of ACTRA Toronto. He is past president of the NDP, and served as national campaign director for the party in 2006 and 2008. He was born in Longueuil, Quebec.

ADAM VAUGHAN is Toronto city councillor for Trinity–Spadina.

MEL WATKINS is a Canadian political economist and activist. He is professor emeritus of economics and political science at the University of Toronto.

RICHARD ZAJCHOWSKI teaches at Camosun College, Victoria, BC, and was one of Jack's best friends for more than fifty years.